From Reindeer Lake

D0762639

From Reindeer Lake

to Eskimo Point

Peter Kazaks

Foreword by George Luste

NATURAL HERITAGE BOOKS
TORONTO

Published by Natural Heritage / Natural History Inc.
PO Box 95, Station O, Toronto, ON, Canada M4A 2M8
www.naturalheritagebooks.com

Cover and text design by Blanche Hamill, Norton Hamill Design
Edited by John Parry and Shannon MacMillan
All photographs courtesy of George Luste
Printed and bound in Canada by Hignell Book Printing, Winnipeg, Manitoba

The text in this book was set in a typeface named Minion.

National Library of Canada Cataloguing in Publication

Kazaks, Peter, 1940 –
From Reindeer Lake to Eskimo Point / Peter Kazaks ; foreword by George Luste.

Includes bibliographical references and index.
ISBN 1-896219-84-5

1. Kazaks, Peter, 1940 – 2. Canoes and canoeing – Saskatchewan, Northern.
3. Canoes and canoeing – Manitoba, Northern. 4. Canoes and canoeing – Nunavut – Keewatin Region. 5. Saskatchewan, Northern – Description and travel. 6. Manitoba, Northern – Description and travel. 7. Keewatin Region (Nunavut) – Description and travel. I. Title.

FC3205.4.K39 2003   917.104'648   C2003-904892-6

ONTARIO ARTS COUNCIL
CONSEIL DES ARTS DE L'ONTARIO

THE CANADA COUNCIL | LE CONSEIL DES ARTS
FOR THE ARTS | DU CANADA
SINCE 1957 | DEPUIS 1957

Natural Heritage / Natural History Inc. acknowledges the financial support of the Canada Council for the Arts and the Ontario Arts Council for its publishing program. It acknowledges the support of the Government of Ontario through the Ontario Media Development Corporation's Ontario Book Initiative. It also acknowledges the financial support of the Government of Canada through the Book Publishing Industry Development Program (BPIDP) and the Association for the Export of Canadian Books.

The wonders of nature are many, but, for me, none are as splendid as Julia, Emily, Karl, Kristopher, Hazen or Maia

Contents

FINAL DAYS: PADDLING HOME

Acknowledgments

OUR FOURTH CHILD WAS TO be born six weeks before my departure, in 1981, for the summer-long canoe trip described here. My wife, Alexandra, knew that I wanted to seize the opportunity, so she eased my mind about abandoning her and the family and encouraged me to grab it. I am very grateful for her support.

I shared an intense experience with my fellow venturers, Gerd Hartner and Dave Berthelet. We depended on each other. Such an adventure forms a bond that persists even in the absence of regular contact. To George Luste, the fourth member of our cluster of humanity in the wilderness, and a friend for over forty years, I owe a special debt. I would not have considered the trip in the first place without confidence in his wilderness skills and his all-round competence. That trust proved amply justified. George inspired me to go and then led us on the trip – which is now among the significant events in my life. Finally, I want to thank the people at Natural Heritage Books, with Shannon MacMillan and Barry Penhale most prominent among them, for making this book a reality.

Peter Kazaks
Davis, California
2003

Foreword

WHY DOES ANYONE WILLINGLY CHOOSE to go on a long and physically difficult wilderness canoe trip? In truth there will probably be as many varied answers to this question as there are canoeists. But I believe that spirituality and escapism are important reasons for many. They are for me.

We are all lonely pilgrims in our passage through this life. During that all-too-brief journey we encounter other wanderers, we share experiences and, from time to time, we seek to connect with something more meaningful and more compelling than the humdrum of everyday living. The great scientist and human being Albert Einstein expressed it thus: "We are all here for a brief sojourn, for what purpose we know not, though we sometimes think we feel it."

The famous Arctic explorer and humanitarian Fridjof Nansen, who won the Nobel Peace Prize in 1922, observed that: "The first great thing is to find yourself and for that you need solitude and contemplation...or at least sometimes.... I tell you, deliverance will not come from the noisy centers of civilization. It will come from the lonely places."

The vast, lonely landscapes of northern Canada provide that solitude in spades. On a long Arctic canoe trip, I escape the consuming concerns of everyday city life and return to the two physical essentials for survival – food and warmth. Time and the wilderness experience reawaken the dying embers within my soul. The endless empty horizons of the Arctic barrens diminish my self-importance. I embrace the consuming solitude, the mystery of life, and give thanks for my existence.

Over the past forty years I have experienced many such canoe trips and seen many northern landscapes – from the Queen Charlotte Islands and the Stikine River in the west, to the Torngat mountains and the rugged coastline of northern Labrador in the east, from the vast glaciers of Ellesmere and Baffin Islands in the north to the rocky shorelines of Kitchi-Gami (Lake Superior) and the Missinaibi waterway in the south. All these experiences have enriched my life. They have, to a large extent, shaped me and my values. For this I am sincerely grateful.

✳   ✳   ✳

In this book, Peter Kazaks relates his experiences and observations on our 38-day trip in 1981 from Reindeer Lake in northern Manitoba to Eskimo Point (now Arviat) on Hudson Bay. The other two members were Gerd Hartner, a physics colleague at the University of Toronto, and David Berthelet, a canoeing acquaintance in the Wilderness Canoe Association.

Do I agree with everything as told by Peter in this book? Probably not, but that is to be expected and of no real importance. The truth is subjective and illusory when it comes to recollection and interpretation. Gerd or David or I, if writing about this same 38-day trip, would probably have differing views on some of the events and interactions. But that makes it all the more interesting.

A first experience is usually special and is, of course, unique. In this regard, Peter's narrative of his first long canoe trip is special. It represents a perspective that I could no longer recapture in my own telling. It reminds me of my own first encounter with the barrens in 1969. That was a unique, intense and difficult experience because there were so many "firsts" for me. Making the same trip a second time would not be the same experience. I think that "firsts" have a special magic about them.

The 1981 journey described in this book was my fourth lengthy venture into the barren lands, following prior long trips on the Dubawnt and Kazan rivers. The Dubawnt trip in 1969 was a tough but memorable introduction to the barrens. My Kazan trip in 1974 was longer and followed J. B. Tyrrell's route and notes north from Reindeer Lake to the Kazan River and on to Baker Lake. All three trips started south of the treeline and finished well into the barrens and the open Arctic. This transition from forest cloak to Arctic bareness is a marvellous experience, as one sheds the comfort of warming fires and the protection of the boreal forest. Best of all is the boundary where the trees are few but sufficient, where portaging is much easier, and hiking the eskers is a joy.

✻   ✻   ✻

At the north end of Reindeer Lake, the Cochrane River flows in from Wollaston Lake. Earlier, in 1974, I had already travelled up the Cochrane River to where one leaves it, on our way to Kasba Lake and the Kazan River. Thus, in 1981, I chose to start out via a different route. We followed David Thompson's travels in 1796 from Reindeer Lake to Wollaston Lake via the Swan and Blondeau rivers. I mention Thompson because I consider him the greatest of all the early traders. In 1916 the Champlain Society published *David Thompson's Narrative of His Explorations in Western America, 1784–1812*, edited by J.B Tyrrell. This is a remarkable narrative by a remarkable human being and I cannot recommend it highly enough. (I stayed up all night reading it after I started.)

Our 1981 travels north did not follow one major river, as many canoe trips do. We changed watersheds a number of times. This, of course, adds considerable physical effort, necessary to portage over the heights-of-land. Why and how did I select the 1981 route? The main reasons are historical. During my prior trip to the Kazan River and down it to Baker Lake I knew I wanted to return to the area. I kept looking at my maps and examining possible routes to the east, between the Kazan and Hudson Bay.

My interest in the historical literature of the area helped. I wanted to visit the Windy River area where Farley Mowat stayed as a young man in 1947, and which led to his writing *The People of the Deer* (1952) and *The Desperate People* (1959) a few years later. I looked forward to retracing P.G. Downes' 1939 route to Nueltin Lake, described so well in his classic *Sleeping Island* (1943). Less well known are the 1912 travels of Ernest Oberholtzer and Billy Magee, who canoed to Hudson Bay via the Thlewiaza River north of Nueltin. In 1925 and 1930 Captain Thierry Mallet, of the Revillon Frères fur trade company, published his two wonderful books, *Plain Tales of the North* and *Glimpses of the Barren Lands*. In 1933, artist Winifred Petchey Marsh arrived at Eskimo Point and provided us with a wonderful folio of watercolours illustrating the local landscape and the life of the people in her book *People of the Willow* (1976). In sharp contrast are the later photographs, by Richard Harrington in his *The Face of the Arctic* (1952), taken of the starvation camps south of the Hudson's Bay Company post at Padlei on the Maguse River. Harrington's powerful images show the dreadful conditions of the Padleimiut people, still clinging to their nomadic lifestyle, after the caribou migrations failed them – a few years before the government finally came to their assistance.

Farley Mowat concludes *People of the Deer* with: "In the days of Inoti, the strength of the great people might be made to live once more, in time it would be our strength, and the people would be our people. And then the dark stain which is the color of blood might at last be wiped from the record of the Kablunait in the place of the River of Men."

It is fitting that the area through which we canoed in 1981 is today part of a new territory called Nunavut, which came into being on April 1, 1999. Nunavut is bigger than Alaska and is governed by the Inuit, who make up 85 percent of the 26,000 people living in 28 isolated towns in a region of tundra, pine forest and ice fields straddling the Arctic Circle.

* * *

In closing, I would like to pay a special tribute to David Berthelet who, on January 30, 1998, lost his fight to cancer and passed away in his 57th year. I remember him with sadness and regret. Sadness because it was only after the 1981 trip that I learned how his marriage and family life had disintegrated at about the same time. He never mentioned this to us during the summer, and I regret that I never really made an effort later to bridge the chasm that developed between us during the trip. He was a good and decent person who, at times, did not cope well with difficulties. Rather than being constructive and sympathetic, I too often simply ignored him during our expedition. I very much regret this now. The only other time I interacted with him following the 1981 trip was in May of 1990 when Herb Pohl and I stayed at his house in Hull, while waiting for our flight north to Pond Inlet. Dave was a gracious host that evening as he treated us to a fine supper. I like to think both of us wanted to somehow make up our differences, but we did not know how to go about it.

I dedicate this foreword to the memory of David Berthelet (1941–1998). I wish I could do more.

George Luste
Toronto, Ontario
September 2003

Introduction

IN 1980, WHEN I VISITED George Luste in his fine old home in Toronto, I went up the dark wood stairway, past the ornate banister and entered the master bedroom. There it was on the wall above the bed – six feet by four feet of yellow and green pastels, splotched with shapes of blue, with a red tendril or two indicating a road pushing up into its southern part. The map of the eastern half of the Northwest Territories dominated the room. I thought, "Boy! George really *is* serious about wilderness canoeing!"

Over the previous fifteen years, George had mentioned his canoeing trips, but we had not spoken of them in any detail, as our encounters had been glancing ones at the conferences that we attended as physicists. Then, when I visited his home while I was passing through Toronto, I spent half a day at his home and found out what canoeing meant to him. Two battered Grumman canoes hung from the side of his house and, inside, photographs and prints of northern scenes and canoeing covered most walls, as did items that he had collected on his canoe trips (such as an embroidered deerskin shirt and a seal skin stretched on a frame). George had told me of his interest in books about canoeing, about the indigenous peoples, about the exploration of the Canadian north, and about how he searched out antiquarian bookstores. But to see his dining room lined with bookshelves and his upstairs den crammed with books all testified more compellingly than any brief account of his could that this was a man devoted to canoeing and to the north.

George Luste and I had been good friends during our high school days in Montreal. Our families knew each other in the Latvian community. We had shared an interest in sports and generally felt compatible. He held back from the beer-drinking sessions and feckless sniffing after girls that preoccupied some of us teenagers. He worked hard in school and in the summers, and he was good at football. That he was somewhat austere only increased the respect in which he was held. We saw each other regularly, even after George went off to Mount Allison University in Nova Scotia while I remained in Montreal to attend McGill University. We both studied at graduate schools in the United States to become physicists. Our meetings became fewer, but we did attend each other's weddings. Our friendship over the years had been a loose and casual one. The old ties briefly rekindled if we happened to meet at a physics conference or I if passed through Toronto, where I had relatives. But we did not write, not even Christmas cards. Because of our friendship as teenagers, we remained comfortable with each other despite the lack of extensive contact.

We had shared what had been the first camping trip for each of us. When we were seventeen, we took a two-hour bus ride north from Montreal to Lac St. Michel des Saints, where we rented a boat with an outboard motor and camped on the lake for three days. Our gear was either crude or non-existent. We made our shelter out of rubberized table covers and pine boughs. I slept in a blanket roll. We spent the days exploring the long bays of the lake. Later George told me that a couple of years after that trip he had been sitting on the shore of the Ottawa River looking at a map when he realized that he could paddle to Hudson Bay in relatively straightforward fashion simply by going downstream on a choice of rivers. So he made a solo trip to James Bay, and it hooked him for good. Now he has become one of Canada's and, therefore, one of the world's, foremost wilderness canoeists.

My interest in the outdoors and in being on the water went back to summer vacations with my family and to fishing with my father at Lac des Isles near Mont Laurier, Quebec, about a hundred miles north of Montreal. For six years we spent two or three weeks each summer at a cabin on the lake. This was cottage country for Montreal, but in the mid- and late 1950s the place was relatively remote and rustic

A rowboat came with the cabin that we rented. Almost every morning my father would go out before sunrise to fish with me or with my brother. We had to be at the decent fishing spots before the sun was up. As the mist rose from the lake, the shoreline was unveiled and the world opened up. If it was calm, I could catch glimpses down into the underwater world;

golden green weeds that we called pike grass reached up from the depths towards the light, coming within two or three feet of the surface. As I cast and retrieved, I would watch to see when I would first glimpse the red and white of the lure as it approached the boat. Occasionally, the hint of a sleek shape would appear behind the lure, followed by a flash of white – a northern pike had followed the lure and then turned away. Sometimes, before I could see anything, I would feel the tug as something live and strong took the lure and fled to the depths. On those calm mornings, as the wisps of fog lifted, I felt that I somehow linked up the world above water and the depths where the fish lived.

Other mornings my father would row as I trolled for lake trout. He wanted his sons to catch the fish. Even heavy rain did not hold us back, and we were usually out on the water on those days too. In summer the lake trout stayed deep, so I would let out plenty of the steel line, as my father rowed. And he rowed for hours while heavy raindrops pocked the surface of the lake.

When I had children of my own, I fitted in day hikes in the Rockies or the Sierras while on family vacations, but I was an armchair adventurer too. I went on a jag of reading about the climbers in the Himalayas, and then I devoured everything that I could find about the mountain men and the first explorers in the American west. I romanticized men such as Jedediah Smith and Jim Bridger – the first Europeans to venture along western rivers. One year, I persuaded my wife, six months pregnant with our second child, and two-year-old Julia to go on an overnight canoe trip in the Adirondacks, and we all squeezed into a pup tent at night. We even did a couple of short portages, with Julia helping by carrying a yellow plastic potty by its handle. Four years later, the four of us had another overnight canoe trip, this time along Fish Eating Creek, which runs through a cypress swamp in Florida. We paddled slowly or drifted. Occasionally we left the creek, which was just a channel through the swamp, to bump along the cypress knees and to get a closer look at the bromeliads in the trees.

But when George told me, when I visited him in Toronto, about some of his trips of six, seven or eight weeks in the remoteness of the far north, of long paddles on enormous lakes, up and down rivers in the tundra, of ice and of rapids, he awakened my interest in an extensive wilderness expedition. The example set by George – and no doubt the approach of my fortieth birthday – rekindled my yearnings. Knowing that George was a veteran northern canoeist, a true expert, I leapt at the chance for a trip with him. George's evident experience encouraged me but – more important – I knew him to be completely reliable and thoroughly competent. He had been independent and resourceful since adolescence, working his way through college at hard construction jobs and excelling in graduate school. He subsequently became one of Canada's prominent high-energy physicists. He takes on tasks with commitment and determination. In short, I trusted him to lead a lengthy, demanding wilderness trip. When we discussed commitments and risks, I, in a plea for caution, begged, "My wife and kids need me." He did not downplay the potential problems but treated the possible dangers and tribulations calmly, as matters of fact, to be treated with care and preparation.

In October of 1980, after returning to my teaching duties at New College in Sarasota, Florida, I wrote George and broached the idea of accompanying him on his next trip. I was delighted to learn that he was already planning for the next summer. But what he had in mind unnerved me – six weeks of paddling through the Northwest Territories, with an extra week reserved for delays caused by wind or ice, and yet another for travel to and from the north. Eight weeks was a daunting prospect; my longest canoe trip had been four days as a counsellor at summer camp more than twenty years earlier. Most of all, I had a pregnant wife and three kids, with a new baby due to arrive in the spring, a month or two before I would leave. But George was not scheduled to run experiments on the big machine at the Fermi National Accelerator Laboratory in Batavia, Illinois, and he wanted to use the time to the fullest in the north.

George reminded me that getting to the launch site and back involved about the same amount of planning, expense and trouble for a short trip as it would for a long trip, so a longer venture was a better investment. Nevertheless, even a four-week trip (my initial hope) in the remote wilderness of northern Canada, without roads and with portages and rapids, blackflies and mosquitoes, seemed very challenging for a novice. I would certainly miss my wife and children, and they could use my help, especially with a newborn. The idea of committing myself to eight weeks of travel through the Subarctic gave me real pause. In an emergency we could easily be more than two weeks from assistance. And if we had a canoe wreck in rocky rapids or one of us broke an ankle on a rough portage, two weeks of paddling might be impossible anyway. The four weeks that I had had in mind began to seem relatively easy.

Why someone would want to forgo the comforts of home and civilization and put up with all sorts of discomfort, gruelling labour and life-threatening danger for weeks on end is a real question. But mountaineers, Arctic trekkers and wilderness canoeists are willing and eager. George does it almost every summer. I wanted to as well – it would satisfy my yearnings and romantic impulses about exploration and wilderness travel. After mulling it over for a couple of weeks, I concluded that such a chance would not occur often. Alexandra had listened to me talk for years of my dreams about wilderness travel, either backpacking in the mountains or canoeing in the north. She encouraged me to go – her mother would come and help with the new baby and the older children. With that support, I made the commitment and, that December, I signed on as the third member of the party of four. Daydreaming had been a lot of fun, but now concrete preparations began, and they too were enjoyable.

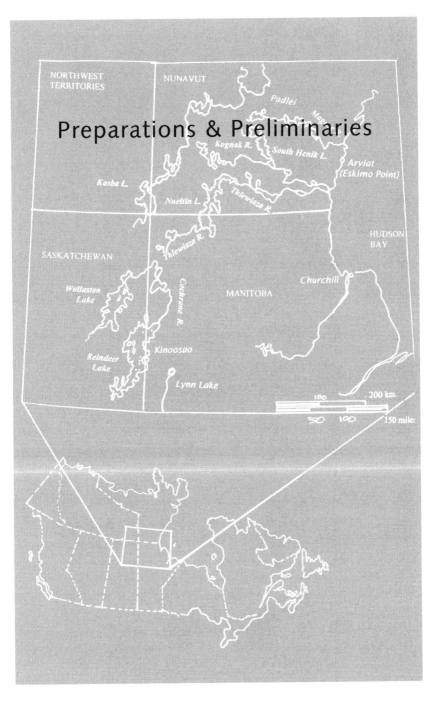

Preparations & Preliminaries

CHAPTER 1

Veterans, Novices and Gear

G EORGE MADE SOME TOKEN CONSULTATIONS with the rest of us but, as our most experienced member by far and the unquestioned leader, he picked the route. He was also the only one who communicated with each of us scattered in Toronto, Ottawa and Florida. We would start on Reindeer Lake in northeastern Saskatchewan, loop north, pass through the extreme northwest corner of Manitoba into Nueltin Lake, which straddles the border with the Northwest Territories (in the eastern part now called Nunavut), then proceed north through a series of lakes and rivers to a latitude of 62 degrees North. Then we would follow the Maguse River east to its mouth on the western shore of Hudson Bay, near Eskimo Point, renamed Arviat in 1996. We would travel in total about 750 miles, the last half of it north of the treeline, in the so-called barren lands of the Sub-arctic. Lakes varying in size from tiny to enormous abounded, and I was eager to go up and down the connecting rivers. But I dreaded the portages – about 25 miles of back-breaking labour.

I began reading what I could find about the north, about canoeing through it, and about the history of the area that we would traverse. The first European in the barren lands was Samuel Hearne, who carried out an incredible overland journey, guided by Natives, in the late eighteenth century. He recorded his four-year trip northwest from near present-day Churchill, Manitoba, to the mouth of the Coppermine River and back, in *A Journey from Prince of Wales Fort in Hudson's Bay to the Northern Ocean*.

But serious exploration of the barren lands is recent. In the early 1890s the Canadian geologist Joseph Burr Tyrrell and his brother, J.W. Tyrrell, carried out the first substantial and recorded exploration of the area during two canoe trips guided by aboriginal peoples. Our trip would roughly parallel their journeys. In fact, George had led a group a few years earlier that closely followed the Tyrrells' journey along the Kazan River. George had particularly enjoyed the park-like country in northwestern Manitoba, and we planned to pass through it again. After that we would travel slightly to the south and east of the Kazan River. George sent me an extensive diary from a colleague on that trip. He also forwarded articles from the *Beaver* magazine describing the barren lands and the Inuit of that region. A photo article of one of George's trips included his poetry, which revealed his awe of the Subarctic, and showed me a side of him that I had not known.

In the first half of the twentieth century the Hudson's Bay Company and the rival Revillon Frères had posts in the area for trading with the Indians to the south and the inland Inuit to the north. The posts are now abandoned: the fur trade is no longer profitable, and the indigenous peoples now live in settlements. Starvation and disease had devastated the inland Inuit. The starvation had begun with the disappearance of the life-sustaining caribou herds and continued with bungled resettlement in the late 1940s and early 1950s. Richard Harrington's *The Face of the Arctic* includes horrifying pictures of Inuit during the starvation winter of 1950 at the Hudson's Bay post at Padlei. We expected that now-abandoned post to be the northernmost point in our trip.

Farley Mowat's book *People of the Deer* and its sequel *The Desperate People* recount the last days of the Caribou Inuit. The first study, set around Nueltin Lake – the mid-point of our trip – describes the plight of the Inuit and the disappearance of their way of life. Mowat captures the excitement of the caribou herds' arrival and of the hunts that twice a year provided subsistence. We, in contrast, are unlikely to see many caribou. The vast numbers simply did not exist any more, and the remaining caribou will probably have migrated northward to their summer grounds.

George also sent me P.G. Downes' *Sleeping Island* – an account of a canoe trip in 1940 from Reindeer Lake to Nueltin Lake that inspired our expedition. I read it avidly – he covered the first half of our route, and his too was a personal adventure with little logistical support. His love of the country and its people is clear. Downes hunted and fished for his food. By contrast, we would have dried foods, reliable maps and modern materials for clothing, tent and canoe. The First Nations gave the name Sleeping

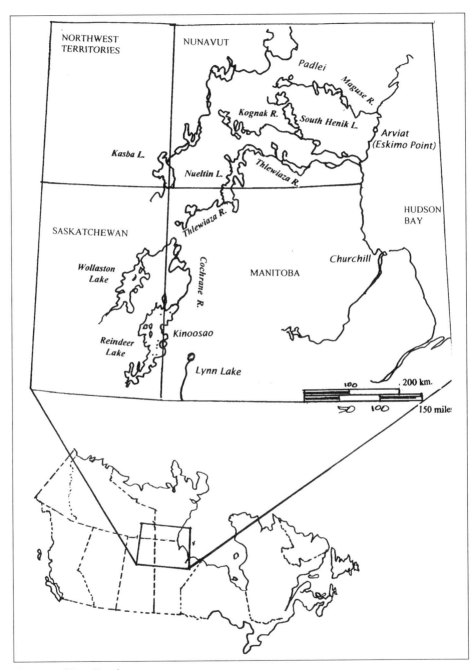

Courtesy of Peter Kazaks.

Island to a lake and an island in Nueltin Lake, and so George and I referred to our Sleeping Island trip when writing each other.

I have always liked to pore over maps before any kind of travel, whether in the wilderness or by car. My brother, Janis, lived in Ottawa and sent me twelve topographical maps from the Canadian Department of Energy, Mines and Resources; most were to a scale of four miles to the inch (1:250,000), and a few were coarser. George obtained some 1:50,000 maps and even, for more difficult areas, the aerial photographs taken for the maps. I spent a couple of pleasant evenings envisioning our route in detail. Where are the rapids? How fast are they? Could we run them, or would we have to carry things around them? Which route will minimize long portages? It is easy to plot a route when looking down at a map, even amid the maze of bays and arms, peninsulas and islands that characterize the north. But, as George had told me and I could easily imagine, when we are on the water, the shoreline could be bewildering. The flat land affords few reference points. A bulge of shoreline seen from the canoe could just as well be a peninsula as an island; a blind bay could appear like the arm of the lake that we are seeking. It would be much easier to navigate in mountainous topography with elevated reference points. I was glad that George was seasoned at this sort of travel.

Food is prominent in descriptions of northern travel. The voyageurs, those engines of the fur trade, ate prodigious meals to sustain their labour-filled 18-hour days. Even so, a voyageur went through marked changes in appearance – the man lying about at a supply post became unrecognizably sinewy a few weeks into the wilderness. In canoe trips of more modern and easier times, the emphasis on meals is still striking. A canoeist's diary entry might read: "Today we covered twenty six miles; the first ten of which were on Lake Daily against a slight head wind. The north end of Lake Daily drains into a river. We had lunch there consisting of peanut butter and peach jam sandwiches and some nuts and tea. We made camp 13 miles down the river. Dinner was our freeze dried macaroni and meats and sauce, supplemented by a roasted pike. Dessert was the freeze-dried banana pudding. And we always had lots of tea throughout the meal. We are by now quite used to the fare but it is quite delicious." In *People of the Deer*, Farley Mowat discusses at some length the necessity of meat in the diet of the First Nations and inland Inuit. He claims that the fat in it is vital. Canoeists and hikers, especially in cold areas, do crave fat-laden meals – fat is tasty (most flavours are fat soluble) and constitutes the most concentrated form of energy. An ounce contains twice as many calories as an ounce of any other food. To sustain a vigorous life in a cold climate without fat would require too much sheer quantity of food.

We could expend up to 4,000 calories a day en route. It would take 8 pounds of fresh fish to supply that amount, or 20 pounds of fruit and vegetables, or about 18 ounces of fat. That is why the voyageurs so favoured pemmican – a mixture half fat and half lean meat, berries or other things, probably including dirt. Since no one wants to subsist on a diet of fat, even supplemented by concentrated protein and vitamins, food provides an endless source of interest, both in planning a trip and in recounting it. I dabbled with food plans, but my colleagues in Canada did the final planning and provisioning. They also arranged for common items of gear such as tents, medical kit, axe and saws. I felt somewhat like a tourist, along for the ride, but I was busy obtaining my personal outfit.

We could expect some extremes of temperature. In *People of the Deer*, Mowat mentions that one mid-June day at Nueltin Lake it was 100°F at noon and below freezing after sunset. Although the heat can be as intense there as in the tropics, the prevailing temperatures will be considerably colder. For example, on George's trip on the Kazan River, the highest temperature on 13 July was 43°F. Loose, layered clothing, the usual garb of people who spend time outdoors, will be most effective. That the Inuit use it is the clinching testimonial.

∗   ∗   ∗

Everything that I read, my own experience, and George's exhortations stressed keeping to a minimum the weight of the gear and, to a lesser extent, its bulk. We would have to carry everything across difficult portages and cram it all into the canoes out of which we would live for seven weeks. We had to determine ruthlessly the necessity of each proposed item and piece of clothing. Then we had to select it carefully, because our safety and comfort depended on it more crucially than does our everyday life on any one thing.

Wool, since it keeps a body warm while soaking wet, was the ideal fabric. A heavy pair of wool trousers (with 15 per cent polyester for durability and easier drying) would be worn all the time. Alexandra made me a pair of rain pants from waterproof nylon. I bought the Gore-Tex jacket that I had always wanted so that I could paddle and portage in the rain. A life jacket, or "personal flotation device," as the jargon goes, was essential. I bought a segmented one to allow for easy movement. Alexandra found two cashmere sweaters at a rummage sale for a dollar each. They seemed luxury items for a rough trip but were so soft that I could wear them next to my skin as undershirts and compact them into a tight bundle. I also took along a T-shirt, wool socks, leather gloves, and, as backup cold-weather garb, a wool turtleneck.

Canoeists are always debating about footwear. Feet and legs are frequently, if not constantly, wet, and light footwear will dry easily. But heavy, firm soles and sturdy boots are essential for portaging and for wrestling canoes through shallows. I went for dryability and purchased two pairs of high-top sneakers – Converse All-Stars, made of double layers of canvas. A pair of wetsuit booties, to keep me warm while wet, turned out to be too light for any purpose except as slippers in camp or canoe.

George, meanwhile, was looking for a fourth person for our trip. We had already signed on a third – Gerd Hartner, a research associate in the Physics Department at the University of Toronto, where George is a professor. Three physicists might be too much of a good thing! Since Gerd also was a novice, someone experienced with whitewater canoeing and the north was essential, so that we might have one veteran in each canoe. George soon found David Berthelet, an economist with the Department of Agriculture in Ottawa. It fell to David and his wife to make most of the arrangements for food. David solved the footwear problem for himself by locating special canoeing boots, then a new product, with heavy soles and a loose-weave fabric that laced up to above the ankle – reasonably sturdy, yet easy to dry. They served him well.

I deliberated about cameras, lenses and film. I had done only casual photography, so I sought advice from a number of people. Finally, George gave me some very persuasive counsel: "I will be taking pictures and have taken lots of them, and Dave will be photographing too," he said. "Since you are basically new to photography and new to expeditions like ours, forget about photography and concentrate on surviving." Thus, all the photos that illustrate this book were taken by George.

I remembered the pain of even trivial portages, so I worked on eliminating as much weight as possible. I decided to take along only one book, for idle moments – probably not many – or while we waited out a storm. Should I take something to remind me of civilization and its refinements and aggravations – perhaps a book by Joan Didion about the anomie of Los Angeles and its freeways? A volume on geology or shrubs and lichens of the barren lands to reinforce what I was seeing for the first time? Perhaps one or two of V.S. Naipaul's books? He does not romanticize the bush; he almost disdains it, and he cherishes urbanity. I decided on John McPhee's *Coming into the Country*, because the subject – Alaska – harmonized with our adventure and his fine writing would be a reminder of civilized life.

I tried to get into condition for the upcoming rigours. My legs and my wind were in good shape from playing full-court basketball three times a week with the students at New College. When they left for the summer in late May, I replaced it with jogging for the month before my departure – three miles four or five times a week. I also started doing push-ups – getting rapidly to 25 repetitions and then staying contentedly at that level. I stood six feet even, and I weighed 172 pounds – six of them excess around the waist. I had once smoked regularly, but had done so only rarely over the previous ten years. I thought that I was in decent shape for a 41-year-old, and well prepared for the trip.

The process of getting the outfit together stretched out in leisurely fashion over six months. I had a tetanus shot and got some dental work done. I gathered other items that might be useful – a crushable felt hat, a head net made by Alexandra with a drawstring for the neck, a spiral notebook and three ballpoint pens for my diary, and press-lock bags for storing maps and for miscellaneous use. Toiletries including a tub of dry skin cream, dental floss, bath jelly in a plastic tube, and a tube of shaving cream. I expected, however, to bathe and shave infrequently up there in the cold among the blackflies. Just before leaving I grabbed a handful of bay leaves from a wreath at home. David Berthelet and the others doing the provisioning would arrange for spices, maybe even bay leaves. But the leaves are light and greatly improve fish chowders and stews – and these ones would remind me of home. And I took along four marzipan bars as a treat for George's birthday, near the end of our trip.

George had a rudimentary medical kit that he had accumulated over the years. We took along an EPIRB, which one activates when a ship at sea is foundering or when an airplane crashes. (There were as yet no satellite phones, which pleases me in retrospect. Our sense of immersion in the north would have diminished if we could communicate to the outside world at will, although I would probably take along one of those phones for safety now.) The EPIRB sends a signal to satellites, which in turn alert rescuers. The problem is to get help to the site in time. I did wonder who bore the expense of such rescues. Why should the public pay to save people who had taken foolish risks? Yet it does cover the costs for careless people – and their victims – in many circumstances in the city and on the highway. At least with the EPIRB, we knew that we would not be completely stranded.

*   *   *

During the months before leaving, I speculated about what we would encounter, about how to approach and overcome difficulties. That anticipation is one of the pleasures of planning an expedition. I knew that the right attitudes and thorough preparation were essential. My daydreaming was also deliberate and purposeful – part of the process. What will it take for our trip to succeed? I knew that we had to be co-operative. Although the inevitable personal differences might be grating, we could not allow them to fester or become inflamed. Personality squabbles could do as much harm as nature.

Physical challenges – portages, rapids, wind and long stretches of paddling – would abound. I knew that we could not rush in, do our damnedest, and hope to conquer them; rather, we would have to adjust patiently to whatever faced us. It seemed clear to me that we would have to approach each challenge and the trip itself with careful thought, deliberation and resolve. I would have to maintain that demeanour even when exhausted, and must not allow myself to become harried. When dragging a canoe up rapids at the end of a long day and enveloped by a malevolent cloud of blackflies, I would still put each foot carefully into the water so as not to sprain or break it. We would need to work hard, patiently and in harmony with each other and with our surroundings. I spent a lot of my idle time thinking and planning and evolved a maxim for success – preparation, prudence and persistence – which I looked forward to sharing with the others.

I knew that I would miss my family terribly, but how much would the remoteness and the isolation from the amenities of civilization, from safety, bother me? One reason for going was to put myself precisely into those surroundings, to experience the wilderness. I wondered how Alexandra, Julia, Emily, Karl and the newborn would fare. Despite the fact that Alexandra's mother was coming for a month, I still had some worries about them and about myself.

One afternoon on a warm day in early May, while Alexandra was resting on a chaise under a large live oak in our back yard, she told me that we had better go to the hospital. We drove to Sarasota and, in less than two hours, Kristopher was born. It was thrilling to witness. Although everything went well and more quickly than the previous births, my opinion that women are the tougher sex found confirmation yet again. Six weeks later, with some anxiety but also with mounting excitement, I flew to Canada to start my first real wilderness trip.

In describing the voyage afterwards, I would start by saying: "Shortly after the birth of our fourth child, I abandoned my wife and family and went into the wilderness for two months." I sported that glibness to assuage my guilt while indicating, if flippantly, my profound gratitude. I remain deeply in my wife's debt for that support and for showing me, by her touching example, how important it is to encourage people to venture forth and to do what they truly want.

CHAPTER 2

By Car, Train and Truck

AFTER SPENDING A DAY WITH my parents and brother Janis in Ottawa, I left for Toronto. I went to the Luste home, where Linda, George's wife, greeted me in her usual cheerful and friendly fashion. Later I met George and, for the first time, Gerd Hartner. Gerd was single, 30, with auburn tints in his brown hair and beard. He was husky, almost oval; George had described him as bear-like – appropriate, if one thought of a modest-sized bear.

After dinner, we did some final packing. George went through Gerd's and my gear to judge whether each item was necessary. One of my sweaters came out, and my fishing rod, with two two-foot-long segments, was still too long and gave way to one of George's rods, which telescoped down to one foot. My plastic bowl, cup and utensils also stayed behind, in favour of communal bowls and cups, which could be nested within each other. Dave and his wife, Denise, had packed each dish of each meal in a plastic bag, combined them into a bag for each meal, and then stuffed these into larger plastic bags. Heavy-duty plastic bags, essential for keeping everything dry, were hard to find, but George had obtained some from a supplier of ornamental gravel.

These bags then went into large green canvas Woods packs, lined with a bag custom made from plastic one-eighth of an inch thick. The Woods packs have leather shoulder straps and a leather tumpline for placing over the forehead during portages. The food bags, which were the heavy, dense items, went into the bottom of our packs, and personal gear on top. Gerd's pack and mine were lumpy compared to George's sleek and taut one, but George assured us that we would soon learn to pack well.

We spent most of the evening in George's study, surrounded by his books on the north, talking about what we would be doing but largely questioning George about other trips, about rapids, canoeing, camping, and the north in general. I also saw pictures of and heard about a three-day training trip that George, David, Gerd and a fourth fellow had taken on a Quebec river for the three of them to get used to each other and particularly to check out their ability to handle rapids. The spring run-off had made the river high and powerful. At one stage, David and Gerd had gotten turned sideways to the current. Then the current had dashed their canoe against a boulder, held it there and bent it into a C-shape. They had photos – impressive and sobering – of the mishap. George had brought out the pictures perhaps to warn me of the power of rapids.

George is usually laconic, imperturbable and business-like. For example, when Alexandra, who is a dietitian and also a fine cook, had asked him the previous summer about the quality of food on his trips, he replied, "You can shove it down." Although he made light of the quality of the food, providing enough was an entirely different matter – as we were to see from the size of the meals on the trip. When relaxing, however, George can banter and joke. That last evening in Toronto even this taciturn veteran showed glimmerings of excitement and anticipation. He ribbed Gerd about the slingshot and the wire snares that Gerd was taking along.

"Why do you want to annoy wildlife, Gerd?" George objected particularly to a .22 rifle. "Even that .22 rifle. Can you hit anything with it? It will be an awkward thing to carry across portages – so if it doesn't annoy any animals it will annoy you. Do you want to dress whatever you manage to hit, and then wait for raw meat to cook?" He concluded, "Really, its weight is not worth the labour, and we have plenty of food."

Gerd agreed not to take the weapon, but they continued jibing at each other throughout the trip. Although neither is loquacious, George and Gerd had a playful relationship. George usually initiated the bantering, but Gerd gave as good as he got. While George and I were discussing our families, Gerd noted, "I guess I am the expendable one if it comes to a crunch. You can sacrifice the single guy."

I learned that Gerd too is an immigrant to Canada, having arrived from Austria in his early teens, whereas George and I were born in Latvia and came aged eight. So by coincidence, all three of us are immigrants as well as physicists.

∗   ∗   ∗

The next day we left Toronto at noon and drove north to Cochrane, Ontario, where we turned west and drove towards Winnipeg. George's ancient Volkswagen van had two canoes on top and our food and packs inside. A platform bed with a foam pad was in the back, and the packs arrayed beside it could serve as a crude bed for someone. At dusk it became chilly, and I shivered as the night wore on. The van had no heater, and as I sat there the cold penetrated me. I began the ride with light cotton trousers and a T-shirt, but by 11:00 p.m. I had on my woollen trousers, woollen socks, two sweaters and Gore-Tex jacket. The temperature fell to 35°F – quite a first night for a Floridian.

We drove through the night, taking turns at the wheel and on the sleeping pad, and kept driving the next morning through rain. The rain stopped in the afternoon, and at 6:00 p.m., after 30 hours of driving, we did too. We were at a campground in a wide part of the median strip of the Trans-Canada Highway, an hour or so from Winnipeg where we were to pick up David Berthelet the next day at the airport.

In the camp Gerd tried out his slingshot on some trees and posts, to the accompaniment of more jibes about the mighty hunter. He joined in, saying that even if he did hit a duck with the slingshot, that would just annoy it. That night George and I slept in a tent, and Gerd, by the luck of the draw, on the bed in the van.

We had breakfast in a restaurant on the highway. Afterwards, in the parking lot, a small car with a Grumman canoe on top pulled up. It contained Ken and Elaine Keyes, each about thirty and acquaintances of George. They would be canoeing for eight weeks in northern Manitoba between The Pas and Churchill. They already knew something about our trip, as did George about theirs. Evidently the fraternity of wilderness canoeists is small.

David's plane was scheduled to arrive at 6:00 p.m., so we went to the Manitoba Museum of Man and Nature in downtown Winnipeg. It contained exhibits about the north, including a full-scale replica of the *Nonsuch*, the ship of the sieur des Groseilliers sent by the British into Hudson Bay in 1668 to explore the possibilities of a northern approach to the furs of the interior. The French at that time dominated the southern approach, from Montreal via the Great Lakes. The voyage of the *Nonsuch*

14

led to the chartering in 1670 of the Hudson's Bay Company, to Charles II's grant to it of some 1.25 million square miles of what is now Canada, and to its towering role in opening and exploiting the fur trade of the Arctic watershed.

After the museum and lunch, while Gerd went to see the movie *Superman II*, George and I rested in a park along the Assiniboine River close to the city centre. I slept on the grass for at least an hour.

At the airport, David, hearty and jovial, greeted us. He had flown to Winnipeg, since even federal employees cannot arrange their time in the summer as freely as academics. We left immediately on our way to The Pas, in the west of central Manitoba, where we were to catch a train next morning for Lynn Lake. David and I got acquainted in the van. He was pleasant, talkative, aged 40 or 41 – the same age as George and I. David was the father of two, had a salt-and-pepper beard, and looked to be of average height, but heavier and stronger. We turned north and continued across the flat farmland. Fearing that no gas station would be open in Dauphin after midnight, we sped on. However, a 24-hour Shell service station greeted us in Dauphin. We refuelled and then drove on, arriving in The Pas in the 4:00 a.m. darkness.

We parked behind a church; Gerd and I slept on the lawn in our sleeping bags, and George and Dave in the van. We had an early breakfast in town three hours later, unloaded the van, tidied up the packs, and loaded them and the canoes on the train for Lynn Lake. George found a person in whose yard we could store the van for the next seven weeks. We did all this in a leisurely fashion, since the train did not depart until 11:00 a.m. As a final step, we stocked up in a grocery store on fruit juice, peaches, tomatoes and a small watermelon for the long train ride. We regarded these provisions with special appreciation – perhaps our last fresh fruit or vegetables for seven weeks.

*   *   *

Mushy, water-logged muskeg is everywhere in this area, including the bed of the railway track. So trains travel very slowly to avoid derailments. The 200 miles to Lynn Lake took about eleven hours. We sat in the only passenger car – completely full – in a freight train. All our travelling companions, many of them children, appeared to be First Nations or Métis,

15

as the people of mixed blood are called. The train stopped at six settlements and gradually the car emptied. Some of the communities are accessible in winter by road, over frozen muskeg, but only train or airplane can reach others. The railway brings mail, goods of all kinds, visitors and returning inhabitants. A bustling and animated crowd of children, adults and dogs greeted us at each stop. It would be a few days before another train from the south, from civilization, came along.

The day was very sunny and the coach became warm. The kids were curious and came around to observe us eating our peanut butter sandwiches and fruit. A vendor sold them large quantities of candy bars, pop, chips and some sandwiches. A large group of First Nations people got off at the last community, leaving the littered coach to us and to a young couple for the last three hours to Lynn Lake. The evening brought clouds, showers and a pleasant coolness, but the prospect of pitching tents outside the Lynn Lake station in the rain was not appealing.

Early in the ride, George and I had talked to a man who had been south to Dauphin to take part in a Métis protest against working conditions at the Canadian National Railway. The Métis had sat on the tracks to block trains and had dismantled some tracks. We had read about the protest in the Winnipeg newspapers. Our seatmate, about thirty and very European in appearance, turned out to be the local leader of the Métis. His replies to our questions were brief to start with, but as our conversation continued, he became more talkative.

"The CNR people are racist. The foremen call us names," he said. "Conditions are bad too – there is only one toilet and one shower in the camp."

"How many people are there?" I asked.

"About seventy."

He was proud that his group had cut a 16-mile winter road through the bush from his village to join with another road. But he complained that the government had done nothing to make it more permanent, that the bush would grow back in cut areas even more rapidly than otherwise, and that it could have been useful but had turned into a make-work project.

We arrived at Lynn Lake about 10:00 p.m., unloaded our stuff from the train and walked a mile into the centre of town to have a beer and find a truck to take us to Reindeer Lake. The local taxi driver claimed that the road was rough and wet and required four-wheel drive. We asked around but found no prospects for a lift.

Lynn Lake is a mining town. We saw all of the downtown and most of the residential area, which is raw, with no landscaping or external ornamentation on the homes. Apparently winters are long and harsh, and the population is relatively transient. Later, I learned that Lynn Johnston, author of the popular comic strip "For Better or for Worse," full of warm and humorous family situations, was then living in Lynn Lake with her dentist husband and two children. Most of the businesses are on the one main street. There are a couple of restaurants, some snack bars, a large grocery – which supplies outlying mines and settlements – and the usual assortment of garages and shops. In rural parts of Canada the liquor-serving establishments are in hotels. Sometimes it seems that the reason for a hotel is to house a tavern, and the invitation, "Let's go to the hotel," means, "Let's have a beer." We went into the tavern and found fifteen or twenty young whites and the same number of Natives sitting on opposite sides of the room. The jukebox blared. We had the beer, in the middle of the room, and left.

We set up tents on the little hill outside the train station. One of the white locals had called the place the "Indians' Hilton." We had been offered space in the baggage room of the station, but it smelled of oil and the concrete floor and the baggage carts were harder than the ground. Engine noises and some kind of mine machinery huffing periodically in the distance lulled me to sleep in the tent and did not bother me during the night.

Next morning we assembled our gear and got it out of the station so that the facility could close at 8:00 a.m. when our train started its return trip south. George went off in the taxi to a nearby lake to drop off the boxes of food to be flown into Nueltin Lake by LaRouge Air. Gerd and David walked up to town to find breakfast and a truck. I sat on the station platform with our packs, waiting my turn for breakfast.

That Saturday morning, June 28, the town was celebrating Canada Day, three days early, with a parade. The occasion marks the establishment in 1867 of Canada (then consisting only of southern Ontario and Quebec, and New Brunswick, and Nova Scotia) as a self-governing dominion within the British Empire. The parade interested us because most of the

17

Dave Berthelet, left, and Gerd Hartner, covered with dust after the truck ride.

trucks in town seemed to be in it. At 2:30 p.m. we arranged for the town's main grocer, whose truck had a large closed box, to carry our equipment. But the box proved not long enough to enclose our canoes, so we would have to keep the door in the back rolled up and open. David and Gerd volunteered to sit in the back, while George and I were in the cab with the driver. I suggested that we trade places halfway. However, when we reached that point, George and I saw that dust blown in from the road now covered Gerd and David, along with our packs. I no longer felt so charitable and argued that there was little sense in all of us getting filthy. Gerd and Dave protested martyrdom, while George and I argued for practicality, but adding some confessions of guilt.

Very few tendrils of road extend into the far north; one of them terminates at Kinoosao on Reindeer Lake. The place consists of nothing more than a large dock and a few ramshackle buildings. Kinoosao is, or was, a shipping point for supplying the Natives on Reindeer Lake and for them to return their fish catch. Most of them live in Brochet, a village near the north end of the 140-mile-long lake, from where they reach the outside increasingly by plane or in winter by caterpillar train.

After our long haul I was surprised to see a few pick-up truck campers parked nearby. But why should they not go where the roads lead, even poor gravel roads? And so there they were – wanting to see what was at the end of the road or just to find how the fishing was. We assumed that they were fishing because nobody was around the vehicles. We unloaded our packs and dusted them off under the skeptical gaze of our driver. He seemed bemused at our folly but interested in our gear. We saw no one else at Kinoosao. The driver wished us well as we loaded our canoes and set off at 5:30 p.m.

✷   ✷   ✷

After all the preparations we were finally venturing out on the water! We would trace out one skein of the immense web of waterways that is the Canadian north. To connect the strands of the web we would have to paddle across lakes large and small and up a series of rivers and down others and haul our canoes and other gear across many portages. We wanted to see the north and to experience life in wild nature. None of us ever said that he went to "seek adventure," but each of us must have been looking for something that we could not find in the comforts of city life or in books about the travels of others. We knew that we would be more immediately and vitally engaged than if we were to drive or fly to some resort. George certainly found something in these trips that made him return again and again. Perhaps the rest of us also desired some kind of fulfillment, unarticulated though it was. As we set out, I felt a tingle of anticipation – and I thought that the others did too – that we would discover answers to all sorts of questions, both explicit and unspoken.

Week One

Finding Our Legs

CHAPTER 3

Bald Eagles on Reindeer Lake

WE WERE FINALLY IN THE water; I was excited and eager – and splashed water with some ungainly paddle strokes. We paddled three miles, a short trip to get us officially under way, to the northeast corner of Moose Island, where we made camp. The evening was beautiful and sunny, with a light onshore breeze and no mosquitoes around the campfire. We settled in on a soft, light green carpet of reindeer moss amid well-separated spruce trees. We had pitched the tents before, but this was our first experience with getting into the packs, breaking out food and cooking gear, cooking with our outfit, and setting up camp in general. We were a bit uncertain about it and relied on advice from George.

Our meal was the traditional first-night feast of one-pound steaks, vegetables and wine, plus the watermelon from the train ride. The steak curved up the steeply pitched sides of our one-quart bowls – from which we were going to eat every day of the trip. After dinner I took a walk on the northwest shore of the island, where a clearing led to a small bay and a tangle of wood that the wind had driven ashore. The sun- and rain-bleached logs choked the entire bay. There I watched the sun approach the horizon. Later we peppered George with more questions about cooking and camp craft, and we speculated again about crossing big waters and running rapids. The evening – balmy, almost without mosquitoes or flies, in a pleasant setting – was idyllic and, for three of us, the start of our first serious wilderness trip!

The next morning we were up at 6 and had grapefruit juice made from powder and a granola rich with nuts and doused with milk, also made from powder. We repacked and were out on the sunny lake at 7. Reindeer was the first of the large lakes that we were to travel; we had to cross the 40 miles of its width in a northwesterly direction and, despite its many islands, numerous open stretches exposed us to much of its 140-mile length. But we were lucky. The lake was glassy in the morning, and we were able to work out our paddling muscles and develop a rhythm. We paddled on one side of the canoe for about an hour and then switched sides to use the muscles on the other side of the body. During the long, open stretches, I had plenty of opportunity to try slight variations of the stroke to ease both my muscles and the monotony. The morning's exhilaration had already given way to routine and even boredom as we entered the large expanse of smooth water in the heat of the day. In fact, the increasing sultriness was the biggest hardship that day.

We crossed the glistening lake through the stillness and heat. As the sun bore down from above and bounced back from the lake, the expanse of flat water became a metallic, light-filled world. We glided on, silently for the most part, and my mind drifted. I looked at the islands in all directions. I thought about what might lie ahead on the trip and about home and city life. Randomly and disjointedly, my mind disengaged itself from the activity – I paddled on in a dream-like state.

A late-afternoon breeze brought relief and even sprinkles of rain. We tried to go from point to point between islands, some separated by as much as a few miles. We became uncertain about which island was which as we approached the western shore of the lake. We went the wrong way around an island and paddled an extra mile or two. The weather was benign, and we crossed the lake that had looked so forbidding on the maps.

After travelling 33 miles, we made camp on the northwest side of a small island near the western shore of Reindeer Lake. The air was still warm, and so were the large rocks on the shore. Everybody bathed, although no one lingered in the 55°F water.

David and I made our first dinner, and I had my first direct encounter with David and his wife's planning and packing. I wondered how many other wilderness diners enjoyed the sort of extensive and varied meals that we had. Each breakfast and dinner was in individual plastic bags. Almost every evening meal consisted of four courses, which meant four bags of dry mix, each of which had to be cooked in a separate pot. The menu that evening was pea soup, millet goulash, potatoes au gratin and date nut squares. Instead of making the dessert, we opened a can of fruit cocktail left over from the feast of the previous day. I had some problems with timing, since each course was not ready when the previous one was eaten. This put out my culinary pride a bit, but I do not think that it bothered the others. I went to sleep tired and content.

We again set out early the following morning. After a short while, we noticed some arctic terns circling and crying over a rocky islet with grass and a few poplars in its centre. We found three nests in the open among the stones. They were hard to spot, since they blended so well with the surroundings. The eggs were dirty grey and mottled with darker spots. Each nest held three eggs, some of them hatched. The newborn chicks, camouflaged in the same earth tones as the eggs, just sat there as the nervous parents circled and screeched overhead.

As we approached the western shore of Reindeer Lake, first one bald eagle and then another, less than a mile later, flew from a perch on a dead tree on a spit of land – sentinels greeting our return to the mainland.

CHAPTER 4

Fire!

WE HAD LUNCH THAT THIRD day at the mouth of the Swan River, a favoured stopping site – we found the remains of fires and an upturned old wooden boat. Chipewyan people had for centuries used the route that we were going to follow – up the Swan and Blondeau rivers and then across a series of portages connecting small lakes to Wollaston Lake.

David Thompson also traversed this section on one of his earliest journeys of exploration, in 1796, going from the Great Lakes to Lake Athabaska, on the northern border between Alberta and Saskatchewan. Thompson travelled on behalf of the fur companies, opening up the country and recording the features of so much of the northwest that he was known as The Mapmaker. He made a number of probes west and north, following many watercourses just to reach the Rockies, where he faced the most difficult terrain of all. He crossed what is now British Columbia to reach the Pacific Ocean in 1811. Among his many accomplishments was the first exploration of the entire Columbia River, including its headwaters. Unlike Lewis and Clark, Thompson had no government sponsor and did not receive the publicity that a nationalistic effort inspires; moreover, he was not one to promote his achievements, so he has not received his due in the rolls of explorers.

This stretch of Thompson's journey that we would follow for the next few days was not physically difficult, but going up small rivers and across a series of very small lakes across a low height of land was a navigational challenge. In some places the Swan River was only 20 yards wide between banks covered with alders, a few birch and the ever-present black spruce. When the river opened up, it became shallow, with expanses of marsh

filled with yellow-green reeds. We glided by the grasses and the trees –
close by, ever-changing, intimate, friendly, and a contrast from the vastness of Reindeer Lake.

Often the river narrowed, and then the current raced and tumbled, occasionally forming heavy rapids. In those places we had to haul and line the
canoes up the stream. Lining was new to me. One person takes a line attached
to the bow and hauls the canoe up the stream while walking the shoreline
or in the shallows. The other person, also walking on shore, holds a line
attached to the stern to keep the canoe aligned with the current but pointing slightly out from the bank by either giving or taking up the line. He can
also push the canoe out with a paddle. The main job of the bowman is to
provide power, while the person in the stern is largely responsible for steering or directing the canoe. If the canoe turns sideways to the current, it can
be swept downstream or overturned. At best all the gear would be wet, but
at worst the gear will be lost and the canoe destroyed, with dire consequences.

Since the shoreline was overgrown and the bank strewn with boulders,
lining was possible only in spots. In the other places we had to jump in
the water and haul the canoe upstream by hand. The canoe still had to be
aligned with the current, but now we pulled and pushed it upstream by
the gunwales. Since the bottom of the waterway was covered with large
boulders just like the bank, footing was uncertain. In some spots, when I
slipped off a boulder I was in water up to my chest. A couple of times as
I floundered in the deep water, I called, "Hold on!" to George, because I
was grabbing onto the canoe for support. And George was holding on to
the bow to keep the canoe from getting pulled out of his hands and swing-
ing downstream. Then I scrambled on the uncertain footing to try to get
under control, with unpredictable results. Usually I tried to find the lighter
spots in the water, which indicated a large boulder upon which I might
step, but sometimes I just gingerly stepped into the dark water, into the
unknown, while holding onto the stern of the canoe. If I went in only up
to my thighs I was lucky. Footing was the main difficulty in hauling
upstream – which is still easier than portaging, at least for short stretches.

If the current is not excessive, and if the shoreline provides good footing, lining is a very easy way to get upstream, but the Swan was a nasty
place to wade in and haul canoes upstream and difficult to line too. The
half-mile of rapids that we ascended, made up of a series of short spurts,

Dave (in front) and Gerd lining up the Swan River.

was arduous but exciting too. The day was warm, the water cool and the experience novel. George did the harder work of taking the bow and pulling. I was grateful for his expertise and received a useful lesson on how to deal with the canoe in heavy water. We had lunch on a large sunny rock in the middle of a rapid.

That evening we sat slapping mosquitoes in our campsite, twelve feet above the water up a steep bank, and watched enthralled as beavers swam around in the still water. Every now and then one thwacked its tail loudly and disappeared under water, then soon reappeared. We had passed a number of dams on the Swan but did not see any beavers until evening.

After having spent a good fraction of the day immersed in the water hauling the canoe, I checked my wallet and found it wet, despite two layers of plastic bags folded around it and fastened down with rubber bands. I opened

A broad stretch of the Blondeau River.

Dave (in stern) as the Blondeau becomes narrower and we approach the forest fire.

everything up, dried it out and decided that it was silly to carry a wallet in my pocket. I had no need of it whatsoever. So I rewrapped it and put it into the bottom of my big Woods pack, where it would stay for weeks.

When we entered Swan Lake the next morning it looked small and friendly in the sunshine. Some parts of the shoreline were rocky, others marshy. We found a rough-legged hawk's nest on a large, isolated rock in the middle of the water. We approached and saw that two of the three chicks were dead. The parents squawked frantically at us, and we soon pushed off. A nearby rock had a seagull's nest on top; two baby gulls swam around it. We paddled further on the lake and reached a rough log cabin. Spruce boughs covered the dirt floor, and the windows were sheets of polyethylene. We could not say whether the trapper had occupied it the previous winter.

From Swan Lake we pushed into the narrow – no more than three canoe lengths at its widest – and tortuous Blondeau River. We probably paddled three miles for each mile of northward progress. After a while the continual direction changing amid the marsh grass seemed wasted effort. We came upon Canada geese that were molting and could not fly, so they scampered along the water in a frenzy to get away. One of them kept just ahead of us

Closer yet to the forest fire. Note that the author's hat is still in fine shape early in the trip.

for some time, terrified that it was being chased. It eventually dove under the water and swam back in the opposite direction to elude us.

In mid-afternoon we noticed smoke rising from a forest fire to the northwest. The plume of smoke was being pushed to the northeast by the wind, and we were heading north. We stopped, looked and made some innocuous comments. Then George said, "Let's keep going," and so we did. But I was nervous and I think that George was too. We kept going until the smoke covered half the sky. It was now apparent that our direction of travel and that of the fire could intersect. But we were not sure about when or whether we would cross well in front of the fire or it in front of us. We thought the nearby small lakes and the narrow Blondeau a sufficient shield, so we pushed on. The smoke became thicker and filled even more of the sky. Soon it was all around us and very thick ahead of us. Finally, Dave and Gerd, in the canoe ahead, called out, "We can see flames!" We pulled the craft to shore and looked about anxiously. Then a gust of wind came up and fanned the fire so that it emitted a deep, powerful roar, like the snarl of a great beast. The back of my neck clenched, and I felt my hair stand on end.

That was enough! "Let's get out of here!" We scrambled into the canoes, turned them around and fled downstream, the fatigue of the long day forgotten. We skidded down four small sets of rapids, occasionally jumping out of the canoe to wade and tug it around the rocks. George and I went first and, after we were through one of the sets of rocks, I heard raised voices and looked back. Gerd and David had lost control after hurrying through the rapids. Gerd was floating in a deep pool and holding onto the canoe with one hand; David also was grasping it, while standing near the stern in shallower water. (Gerd's lifejacket was on, as were ours most of the time.) I heard Dave say, "I'm captain of this bloody ship. When I say go left, go left!"

We continued our scurry downstream, Dave and Gerd silent and grim-faced. Our canoe was silent too, and I wondered if this would be a serious crack in our so-far harmonious trip. A while later George suggested, "Gerd, why don't you and Peter change canoes for a while?"

"No. We'll stay the way we are," Gerd replied.

We remained the way we were and continued downstream. I had been apprehensive about approaching the fire and crossing its path. I now

32

Author Peter Kazaks, George and Dave the day after the forest fire.

thought that we had assumed too much risk. When the other canoe was out of earshot I spoke to George.

"George, we have families. We shouldn't be trying to outrun forest fires. When we do stuff like this we should also think of the people back home."

"It's not that risky." George said. "If we wait for the fire to pass, we could be held up for a week, since the fire would smoulder and could be fanned into new life by a wind. I'm worried that that is exactly what might happen now, now that we have been driven back."

Well, we're safe for the time being, I thought, but it still seemed risky.

We went about five miles downstream, back through the rapids up which we had laboured. We camped on a high esker with our canoes in the muddy bank of the Blondeau below. On the other side of the esker a narrow lake afforded some protection from the fire, should it approach. I thought the waters too small to be of much good in a major conflagration. But the wind did not shift; it died down. And so did the plume of smoke in the distance – and our fears.

We were tired, our nerves were strained and the mosquitoes were out in greater force than earlier. Dave said that he needed a drink, but I am not sure if he even took a drink from his quart of rum. In setting up his and George's tent, he did rip the zipper near the corner of the entrance. George had emphasized that a loss of equipment or breakdown could be serious out where no replacements are available. But the small opening at the torn zipper could be patched or blocked off, so it would probably not be much problem in heavy bug areas.

The next morning brought a lift to my spirits, despite its being overcast and our having to go up again through the sequence of rapids and then through the fire area. It was becoming plain that I liked all aspects of the trip. I enjoyed being out in the wild; I was eager to see what each day and each hour would bring.

We were soon past the sets of rapids and entered the burned-out area. Smoke rose from embers here and there; the ground had been blackened and smoothed by the fire. The trunks of the spruce stood like exclamation marks, stark and emphatic. We posed for photographs, as if in triumph over the fire or over our anxieties of the previous day. The devastated area extended for almost a mile on both sides of the Blondeau River.

CHAPTER 5

Beasts of Burden

W E KEPT GOING PAST THE burned-out district and began to look for the portage to the chain of small lakes and portages that would take us over the height of land to Wollaston Lake. People who had canoed there in the previous five years had told George about a log house that marked the start of the route. After considerable searching we found a caved-in log house in a bay on the west side of the Blondeau. Two centuries earlier, when portages had heavier use, David Thompson perhaps found them more easily. Native guides would certainly have been of great help then.

Two-thirds of a mile was rather long for our first portage, but a good, firm path made it relatively easy, and then a light, cooling rain began to fall too. Portaging is plain hard labour, but not too difficult if the footing is good and the distance not too long. As much as one mile along a smooth, level path, and in a gentle, cooling breeze that keeps the bugs away, is tolerable even when you carry 75 pounds – the weight of our canoes and of our full packs. Each person had to cross each portage twice, with canoes and six large packs making up the bulk on each trip.

Each of us had a Woods pack filled with food and personal gear and a small day bag for items of daily use. There were two other large communal packs – a Woods carried food, and a backpacker's (with an aluminum frame) carried pots, utensils, kitchen gear in general and more food. Two taut, cylindrical tent bags held our four-man Eureka Timberline tents. Our communal lunch bag was stuffed with jam, peanut butter, margarine, honey, powdered juice and tea, and mixtures of nuts and dried fruit. Before lunch it held a two-pound loaf of bread. We baked bread in a reflector oven every two or three days. Each morning we put a loaf in the lunch bag and replenished the other items in it as needed. George and David each had a camera case. Finally, there were eight paddles.

Although George carried our canoe on most portages, I did take it occasionally later in the trip. It was cumbersome, especially on uneven ground or in a breeze. I generally transported the kitchen pack and my Woods pack. I usually took the lunch bag on top of my Woods pack on the first crossing, resting it on top of the Woods pack on the back of my neck. On the second traversal I would carry the kitchen pack with the tent on top. On one or other of the carries I would sling my personal daypack around my neck so that it hung in front. Its five pounds was enough to unbalance the body, so I did not want it in one hand. I would take the two paddles by hand and use them as canes amid boulders or in boggy stretches.

The Woods packs are large canvas bags with leather shoulder straps. Each has a tumpline strap, two and a half inches wide, for placing across the forehead, so that the neck muscles can relieve some of the load from the back. They have been in use in the north country for a long time. Some canoeists favour them, perhaps because the voyageurs used them, to carry loads well over 100 pounds. They can hold a lot of gear, but the aluminum frame packs used in backpacking and hiking are easier to carry. The Woods packs sit lower on the back and have no waist strap to provide support above the hips.

One of the hardest tasks in portaging is to stand up when starting out. Usually I sat down in front of the heavy pack, with the smaller items arranged nearby. Then I fitted myself into the pack harness and tried to rise by turning, getting on my knees and pushing up, and at the same time gathering the smaller items. After tottering and straining I felt relief to be standing upright. But, after a few steps, as the load settled in and muscles and joints felt the stress, any relief was dispelled by consciousness of the massive downward load. Then, after more steps, awareness of weight was replaced by pain, and eventually by agony as I just concentrated on the next step. And if it was the first trip, you knew that a second carry would follow. A portageur is a beast of burden, plain and simple.

Most of the portages that fifth day were short, and many routes were easy to find – wide cuts cleared for snow tractors that supplied the Native villages in winter. We traversed nine portages totalling about four miles. The longest was a killer, not because it was one and a quarter miles long, but because one-fifth of it was through bog. We were frequently in the cold muck up to our knees. One foot would sink into the mud as I put weight on it, and I would pause and pull the rear foot out and step forward with it to begin its slow immersion, and so on. We tried to step on the higher hassocks of grass that stuck out above the bog. Sometimes the foot just slipped and then, loaded as we were, we lost our balance and fell in the muck. I went down on one knee a number of times. Once I fell forward on my hands and knees. To get back upright with that heavy load was a real chore. Gerd fell backwards and looked like a turtle unable to right himself.

With each step on that portage my neck hurt and my back protested. I leaned forward and concentrated on each step; occasionally, when looking up to pick my path, I would see my partners in the distance going about their own grim labour. I gasped for breath and cursed the bog and looked for somewhere to place my foot next. Sometimes I propped the butt of the paddles under my armpits and used them as crutches to lean slightly forward to have a short rest. If I sat down or put down the packs, it would require too much effort to get them back up again. Nobody could pay me enough for such labour, yet here I was doing it for fun. I did place the first load down approximately halfway across the portage, but past the bog, and went back, light and relieved, almost floating, to carry the second load all the way. On the way back to retrieve the first pack I discovered a common perception on portages – the leisurely amble back seemed longer than the monotonous grind of carrying a load. Probably concentrating intensely on each laborious step makes past and future evaporate; only the present, which has no duration, exists. The end of the portage was an enormous relief, like reaching a promised land. Although the immediacy and sharpness of the excruciating labour receded, the grim memory lasted longer. Whenever we approached a portage I prayed for decent footing, dreading mud or rough, uneven rocks

We ended that fifth day on the east shore of Compulsion Bay, the southeasternmost arm of Wollaston Lake. According to the maps, we had ascended 200 feet from Reindeer Lake to reach Wollaston Lake which, at 1,306 feet above sea level, was the highest elevation to which we would canoe. It was tempting to think that the rest of the voyage would be a downhill run to the sea, but that of course was far from the truth. We had covered less than one-tenth of the total distance – more than 700 miles was still to come.

CHAPTER 6

Wollaston Lake

WOLLASTON LAKE IS UNUSUAL IN that it drains in two directions. At the north end, some of its waters flow through the Cochrane River to Reindeer Lake and then south; on the west side, the Fond du Lac River also drains the lake northwestward, taking the waters eventually to the Arctic. The bed of the lake is a bowl in a gently sloping saddle that lies on a wide height of land not much above the surrounding territory.

We arrived at 9:30 p.m. after a hard day – too late and tired to look for a good campsite. We settled for one on a peninsula burned over some years earlier. Foot-high saplings of birch and spruce abounded. But plenty of charred wood lay about, and we had to work to keep clean. Despite the late hour and tiredness, George kept us disciplined by insisting that we bake bread – we could not let supplies get too low because we might face a real emergency. So that night I made my first attempt at baking in the reflector oven.

I had learned the rudiments from watching George two nights earlier. We would mix water with the pre-packaged bread mix in our largest kettle and, when the dough cohered, it was taken out and kneaded, usually on the plastic blade of a paddle. Then we would shape the dough and place it in two oblong baking pans. The pans were then set in the reflector oven. When the crust on the side of the fire had browned, we turned the pans. When the whole loaf was a rich brown, it was removed from the fire. But that night, since I finished in the darkness, it was hard to judge the colour. Timing the turning and removal is the tricky part.

At the campsite we talked about the portaging and the killer bog. We griped and groused, yet revelled in the difficulties overcome.

"What do you do to keep in shape during the winter?" George asked me. "You handled the portages quite well."

I was pleased – a novice receiving a compliment from a veteran. "Well, I play basketball three times a week with the students – pick-up games that get pretty serious sometimes. Then in June, after the students left, I did some jogging and push-ups for this trip. What do you do in the winter?"

"Nothing. I just let the trip get me in shape," George replied. "After a week or two I hit my stride. Maybe something from the summer before does last through the winter, but I do gain weight."

Dave and Gerd had also done only casual exercising before the trip.

The last two days had been tough ones, with a lot of work up and down the rapids and across portages. They had also been long days, starting in the water at 7:00 a.m. and making camp at 9:30 p.m. I was relieved to reach camp, but then other chores still faced us – unloading canoes, setting up tents, cooking, baking and washing dishes. That night we went to bed at midnight and decided to recuperate by sleeping late and having a leisurely morning.

Arriving at Wollaston Lake after a series of portages. From the left: Dave, Gerd and Peter.

39

✳   ✳   ✳

The next day was warm and sunny as we headed north on Wollaston Lake. We ate lunch on the large, flat ledges of a rocky island and tasted the bread that I had baked. Hearing no compliments, or at least not waiting for them, I offered, " Pretty good bread."

"Hmmm, it's not well enough done." George was ready to start a baking rivalry.

"This tastes better since it is more moist, not dry and crumbly," I replied, but I knew that it had just happened to turn out that way.

"But it should be able to keep for five days or even more, and since we bake with no preservative, yours might spoil," George rejoined.

And the two of us kept up a bit of a baking competition, or at least a bragging contest, for the rest of the trip. Sometimes we extolled the extras that we added – diced orange peel, raisins, sunflower seeds. Once I said,

Gerd, Peter (with a hat beginning to look bedraggled) and Dave having lunch on Wollaston Lake.

"You guys are lucky. This batch of bread has extra protein. I kneaded a dozen or so blackflies into it. They seemed to be offering themselves up as sacrifices."

"I wish they committed mass suicide away from camp," Gerd said.

✶   ✶   ✶

We were deep in Canadian Shield country, forested mainly with spruce and dotted with thousands of lakes, many with rocky shorelines and some sandy beaches. The Shield is an enormous triangle of mainly igneous rock that underlies everything from the mouth of the Mackenzie River in the western Arctic to Wisconsin in the south and Quebec in the east. We would soon be travelling through its treeless regions. What really characterizes this worn, ancient rock, dating back more than two billion years to Precambrian times, is the endless array of lakes and rivers that ice sheets and glaciers have left behind.

We stopped on another island to explore a trapper's cabin. This one was something of an establishment, consisting of a tent cabin, two doghouses, a pole teepee for smoking meat, and a main cabin of three rooms. The living room/kitchen held an iron stove. It was partitioned partially from a bedroom with one bed. The back room had two beds. All the beds as well as the roof were made of peeled spruce poles about two inches in diameter. A lot of work had gone into constructing the place. A child must have lived there: one of the beds was smaller, and a plastic pistol lay on a shelf, as did a ten-inch-long snowmobile carefully crafted by hand from wood and tin. Pages from a calendar from a Catholic church in La Rouge, Saskatchewan, were torn down to December of the previous year. Postcards from Catholic shrines in various parts of Canada were on the wall.

A few shirts and a couple of cloth jackets with hoods were scattered inside the tent cabin and in the main cabin. Outside we found parts of snowmobiles, a hatchet, a saw and some traps. A moose skull lay in the bushes nearby. The place was clearly more than a crude trapper's camp. I wondered how many winters the family could snowmobile or fly in for trapping before the youngster would have to go to school – or would they themselves teach the child? By living in the trapper's camp, the kid could learn things about nature, animals and survival in the bitter northern winter that he or she could not learn elsewhere. But they would all be cabin-bound for months.

In the afternoon we took advantage of a southerly wind and tied a tarpaulin to two paddles and held it up between the canoes. We sailed for three miles on the sparkling lake past wooded shores – a nice break from paddling. While we relaxed and scudded before the wind, the others, sitting behind me, commented in wry admiration on the blackfly bites that speckled the back of my arms. The previous day I had been the only one to portage in short sleeves, and each bite was now red and inflamed. Camp that evening was on the shore, just east of Gow Island, where Wollaston Lake opens up into a sea-like expanse.

We had travelled approximately 100 miles in six days but had covered about five miles – near the fire – three times. In that 100 miles we had seen plenty of variety: more than thirty miles on glassy smooth Reindeer Lake, hauling the canoe up rapids while wading or while lining it from the shore, paddling in confined waters, grim portaging, and scrambling from the forest fire. We had seen a couple of trappers' cabins but not another human being, not even any boats in the distance. We were getting our camp routines under control. Packing and unpacking took a lot of time, but we were becoming efficient. We were accustoming ourselves to canoeing and to camp craft. Most of all I exulted in being outside, to living in the isolated north. I could not wait for more.

✶   ✶   ✶

Next morning we were back in the canoes at 7:15. After going three miles to the northeast, we stopped at Wollaston Lake Post just to make contact with people and to look around. Most of the buildings were prefabricated government housing for the Cree population of the lake. We arrived before anyone was up. As we walked in the bright morning sun up the centre of the only road in the silent village, I felt as if we were four *hombres* in a spaghetti western swaggering up the middle of the town. I still had on my leather gloves and my felt fedora, by now quite shapeless, and a knife on my belt, but Clint Eastwood did not appear.

Three small airplanes and a number of twenty-foot boats were at the docks. Fishing nets hung near the houses. A co-op store, a government health clinic, and a fish-processing plant formed the core of the town. Most prepossessing was a playground for Cree children, who probably come from some distance to board at the school there. Since there is no road access, they must come by boat, plane, or snowmobile during the school year. The playground had ramps, climbing jungles and cabins, all made of logs two feet in diameter. An old fishing boat, complete with enclosed cabin, had been hauled out of the water and refurbished, and now served as a playhouse.

By the time that we had circled the village, some Cree men carrying lunch boxes were on their way to the fish plant. We nodded to them, and they returned a curt nod. We knew that not many canoeists showed up there – one party a year at most. The men seemed reserved and, at any rate, were on their way to work, so we did not approach them but instead returned to the canoes. We too had to labour, as we had to cover quite a few miles of open water.

The day continued sunny and the occasional breezes aided us. The middle of the day was warm, but when a breeze sprang up or the sun went behind a cloud it was just exhilarating to be on the lake. The clear, crisp air made details on the shore and the play of distant water appear near and distinct. We paddled in an unlimited expanse of enormous sky and open water. The changing pattern of islands and shore textured our world, and it was our world – no sign of humanity was visible – and we were vitally in it. Later, when I came across a collection of nature writings gathered by Scott Slovic and Terrel Dixon, I thought that their title, *Being in the World*, could not be more apt; it resonated profoundly.

As the afternoon progressed, the sun became more oblique and glinted off the ripples of the lake. Above, scattered tufts of cloud added variety and texture to the blue sky. I dug the wooden paddle into the water and pulled with such zest that it flexed. Lean forward, dig in, pull, feel the shaft flex, feel it spring back and help propel us, complete the stroke, and do it again. We went across most of the open expanse of Wollaston Lake that day. In the cool of the late afternoon, as we neared the islands in the northern part of the lake, their features became larger and more distinct, as if welcoming us. A great paddling day! I must have reached paddling shape. We had put another large lake behind us with no trouble. I thought that French horns should herald our approach to the north end of the lake.

*   *   *

Only two weeks earlier I had delighted in a concert at Van Wezel Hall in Sarasota. What a piece of work is man! Here I was exulting in hard work

43

and living in pristine and primitive wilderness, while only a short while ago I – the same person – had been enjoying the most refined accomplishments of high culture. To listen to music in a concert hall – designed to provide acoustics and visual aesthetics and built to hold 1,500 people and 80 musicians who have trained for years on instruments that represent the epitome of craft, all to hear or perform a composition by some individual with extraordinary sensibility that can evoke the most profound emotions – is to relish and honour the accomplishments of our culture. But the same concertgoer can also live in the land and toil across its surface by primitive means. In each of those activities – enjoying the refined accomplishments of our fellows and living in nature – we are connecting to our essential selves.

All sorts of ruminations passed through my mind during our long paddles. Paddling for long stretches is work but, for someone used to it, not much more difficult than walking. After a couple of hours a familiar ache appears between the shoulder blades with each stroke. Sometimes it is a gnawing ache; at other times a sharp sting at a certain point in the cycle. George says that the pain never disappears while one paddles, although shifting the stroke slightly can change its nature. By then I had paddled enough to have a small ache in my seat, which is planted on the canoe seat all day and forms the point about which the upper body pivots during each stroke. To cushion the aluminum seats and to insulate them, George had provided pads made of closed cell foam by cutting up an old sleeping pad.

Every hour or so, we shifted from paddling on one side of the canoe to the other side. Whoever wanted to relieve a set of muscles would say, "Let's change," and we would shift. I also made small adjustments of the stroke because some minor ache might be bothering me. The paddling itself was not much of a problem, but I discovered what encumbrances the feet and lower legs are during long stints. I did a lot of twitching and shifting to find a more comfortable position, particularly for my feet and legs. I tried bending my legs back under my seat, either straight back or crossed at the ankles under the seat. I tried extending the leg opposite the side on which I held the paddle, with the near leg bent back under the seat or flopped around in various positions. No one position was entirely comfortable for long. I thought that if canoeists had evolved only for paddling, they would have no feet at all and only vestigial lower legs. This way they could still do power strokes – in which one shifts the weight that is mainly on a leg extended forward back to a knee placed on the bottom of the canoe – and they would also be comfortable in long-distance cruising.

We made camp at 6:45 p.m. on Usam Island on the pretty channel that leads to the Cochrane River. The campsite, fifteen feet up a steep bank in a grassy clearing among small spruce and poplars, faced the evening sun. We relaxed after paddling 37 miles. A slight breeze kept the mosquitoes and blackflies away.

In a sandy spot along the shoreline I saw wolf tracks and wondered if a wolf had seen us and perhaps was even now watching from across the channel. I was disappointed that we had not seen any bigger animals – plenty of birds such as terns, gulls, geese, ducks and some eagles, but no large wildlife. The caribou were north, well above the treeline, at this time of summer. This land does not support much wildlife anyway. It was mainly mature black spruce forest, with not much diversity in vegetation. As we inched northward, however, the trees could not survive the bitter cold and wind of winter, and they would become sparse and scattered. At this point we were entering the transition zone where black spruce forests gradually gave way to the treeless tundra.

We basked in the sun and casually set up camp.

"Well, we made it," I said. "Those two big lakes were not too much trouble."

"Yes, we were really lucky with the weather," George replied. "A decent wind coming across a half-mile stretch can pin us down, so you know what could have happened on these open waters. I've had to sit for a week on lakes like this."

It was David's and my turn to cook. I started arranging rocks for a fireplace while David gathered wood. Then David and George finished the fireplace while I mixed and kneaded the bread. David's and my cooking partnership had quickly evolved so that I did the cooking and he the dish washing. I made creamed corn soup and instant chocolate pudding to hold us while the beans cooked. For dessert I prepared blueberry pudding cake, modifying to our circumstances the instructions from Denise, David's wife, "Add 3/4 cup of water to bread mixture and mix well, spread evenly in bottom of pan. Pour blueberry mixture on top and add 3/4 cup of hot water. Put that pan inside another one which is half full of water; cover and cook for 55 minutes at 350°F." I cooked the one pan for about half an hour over whatever temperature the fire provided, and it tasted fine.

David had developed a blister on his foot two days earlier during the portage to Wollaston Lake. Since he was a bit lame, he asked Gerd to fetch a pail of water from the lake for washing dishes, and Gerd kindly complied. After dinner David again mentioned his foot and asked, "Peter, why don't you wash the dishes for me tonight and I will owe you one?"

I paused a bit while weighing proprieties and then asked, "Why don't you just hobble around and finish off the dishes?"

And David did so without complaint. I thought that I had done my work and that each of us should continue to bear his load. Yet David was probably not delighted to see me lolling around, leaning back against a pack and smoking an after-dinner cigar while he limped around doing the dishes.

⋆   ⋆   ⋆

The following morning started out a little cloudy but soon turned sunny again. After a short paddle we came to a deserted village of 15 to 20 well-constructed log cabins near the shore in the spruce trees. The peeled logs were still yellow and gleaming, indicating recent building. Indeed, the village, on the west side of the channel opposite Usam Island, was not on our maps. Caribou antlers, legs and hooves lay strewn about on the ground. We knew that caribou moved down south for the winter to this vicinity, and we thought that this was perhaps a wintering place for the Cree. Where they had gone, probably for the summer, we had no idea; perhaps they were still just 40 miles south on Wollaston Lake, at the settlement that we had passed.

We paddled a couple of miles further and stopped to look at a high esker opposite the northwest point of Usam Island. As we approached the shore, the water became very shallow, and I groaned to myself at the prospect of getting my sneakers wet – they had finally dried – when I would have to jump out and haul the canoe up on shore.

"Let's pull around the corner where the water is deeper and we can step right out on shore," I suggested. "We've got to save my dry feet."

Gerd, sympathizing, said, "Bloody Indians should put up docks."

I laughed, and George replied, "Why don't you make that your project, Hartner – putting up docks throughout the north?"

Week Two

On the Tundra

CHAPTER 7

Esker Country and the Cochrane River

E SKERS — LOW, LONG, NARROW HILLS akin to levees that meander — are prominent topographical features in the generally flat north country. They range from fifteen to eighty feet high and sometimes stretch for as much as twenty miles. They were formed from the gravel that collected in rivers that ran within glaciers. As the glaciers began to melt, streams formed in them and gathered up the collected gravel debris. On a detailed topographical map, eskers look like caterpillars. Their tops, gravelly and easily shedding water, have few trees or brush and provide good footing, so many of them have animal trails along their spines. They are the highways of the north.

Our nearby esker branched into a Y and formed a peninsula overlooking a widening of the channel at the north end of Usam Island. We again saw wolf tracks in the sand as we climbed to the top. Prevailing winds had sanded over the fork at the tip of the peninsula to form a wide beach. Behind the beach was a marshy pond within the Y-shaped esker. We were too far north for much vegetation and the esker simply did not support much growth. The light green grasses of the marsh contrasted with the swatches of sand on the hillside and with the clusters of birch and spruce. Silver and green caribou moss covered much of the sand. The place resembled a landscaped golf course with plenty of sand traps. The day was sparkling. Green masses of islands and the distant shore stretched across the skyline. This was my first sight of the esker country, and I understood why George had extolled it.

We paddled a few miles across the open water and made a stop at noon on an inviting sand beach on the north end of Wellbelove Bay. This was

48

to be a short day – of rest, bathing, washing clothes, hiking and catching up with writing our diaries. After lunch I wrote my log while the others bathed and napped. When I finished writing, I was too restless to nap so I went for a hike along the esker at the foot of which we had camped. I sauntered for more than a mile over a variety of mosses and through sparsely placed trees, but with an occasional thicket that I had to go around. The caribou moss – a lichen – was either pale green-yellow and so dry that it crackled when I walked on it or softer and mainly yellow. Sphagnum moss, soft and moist, is an entirely different species of more southerly latitudes, but some was also growing here, frequently in the shade. Expanses of these pale yellow and green pastels carpeted the countryside, studded with spruce, some birch and the occasional poplar.

A pair of eagles were flying above the esker. They made a few passes, flew to within 15 or 20 yards of me and then, when they had a good look, recoiled. Eventually they circled at varying distances, even as close as 20 yards, and made soft, low-pitched clucking sounds. They seemed

An esker on the Cochrane River.

distressed; I must have been near a nest. Or they may have been eyeing me as potential carrion.

On returning from the hike, I bathed and washed my T-shirt and under-wear. The others were still asleep. I made a small fire to heat water for shaving. This was my second shave since leaving Lynn Lake eight days earlier. I had tried once before, during a lunchtime swim on Wollaston Lake. I had stood in the water up to my waist, lathered up with cold lake water and soap, and bent over trying to see my reflection in the water. This time I again shaved without a mirror, but I had hot water, took my time and made a reasonable job of it.

I had worn only one set of clothes thus far – the same underwear, socks, trousers and T-shirt. These had all become wet while I hauled the canoe up rapids – and had thus been washed to some extent. I had deliberately washed my underwear and T-shirt once. On this day they dried on a bush while I wore my wool pants and cashmere sweater. My socks, well soaked most days, were very clean. Some days I put on my Gore-Tex jacket in the morning and evening in camp to keep off the wind and mosquitoes. At night my pyjamas and sleeping bag were more than comfortable.

The lifejacket was proving extremely useful. It had already served as a vest to keep me warm when it had been chilly and windy on the water. But it could also be a pillow at night and a cushion to ease seating or lying around on rocks in camp. We usually kept a lifejacket on during paddling as a safety precaution even during calm periods, but not always. Sometimes it was just too warm to paddle with a lifejacket and a T-shirt. When we took it off it was always right next to us, perhaps right behind us in the canoe. Paradoxically, I sometimes put it on during a lunch stop, because the cessation of paddling made the breeze feel colder. I became very fond of it, especially when lolling about on rocks or snoozing briefly after lunch. Our gear – equipment from the civilized world – became dear to us as it proved its usefulness over and over again, especially when we realized that it could not be replaced.

After bathing and shaving, I tried fishing for the first time on our expe-dition. Earlier I had not had much time or inspiration, but now I had no luck; the bay was shallow, with a sandy and stony bottom. We had supper, and then the other three – the afternoon nappers – went off on a hike while I resumed writing in my log. This was a very fine day of rest; it happened to be July 4! I had become utterly at ease in the canoe and in camp and was luxuriating in the trip.

*　　*　　*

The next morning was bright, but a strong wind blew from the northwest. We paddled a couple of miles before deciding not to buck the headwind. We noticed a large cabin made of plywood sheets and wall panelling on the west shore of the Cochrane River and stopped there to wait out the wind. It was the only white man's cabin that we had seen or were to see between Wollaston Lake Post and the fly-in fishing camp where we were to resupply on Nueltin Lake. Sandy hills, or eskers, surrounded the structure and we could bask in their lee sides and enjoy the views of the water and islands all around.

While the others enjoyed the scenery or just lay about, I took my fishing rod and hiked south to a sheltered lagoon. On the way I tried a few fruitless casts with the red daredevil lure into the main body of water, the Cochrane River, which here stretched six miles across to the east shore of Wellbelove Bay. The lagoon, however, had plenty of small pike to entertain me. I walked around the west side, catching pike or getting bites. Some followed the lure in but did not bite; others I shook off the hook before landing them. A few I had to unhook before releasing. Submerged logs were all about and I snagged a few, and so had to wade in and work my lure loose. I did keep a two-pound pike along with a one pounder, which had taken the hook too deeply to be released.

I cleaned the fish back at the canoes, fried them over a small fire on the shore and then carried them and our lunch bag up the hill to the cabin where the others were lounging. We did not have salt for the fish in the lunch bag and did not want to extract it from our large bags down on the shore. At least that was our excuse for entering the cabin through a window – breaking in – although curiosity was the real reason.

So we had our lunch indoors, in the large living room/kitchen, on actual furniture around a central firepit made of bricks and open all the way round, with a metal hood and ducting above. In addition to the salt, we took some toilet paper and four potatoes. Our rationale was that we were saving the potatoes from the fate that a lemon had suffered when it had rotted near the sink. The cabin was large, containing four bedrooms, each with two double bunk beds – probably a corporate fishing and hunting camp.

After our meal we went back outside – we did not want to linger on somebody else's property, and anyway we were by now so used to the outdoors that we preferred the open air. We languished in the shade, trying to nap and waiting for the wind to die down. It did die in the evening, so we left quickly at 7:00 and knocked off sixteen miles before making a camp at 11:00 as the sun began to set.

The campfire was on a granite shelf on the east shore of the Cochrane. We pitched the tents a few yards inland. The large flat rocks were convenient for lounging on and viewing the sunset. Even at midnight, Gerd could see well enough to sew on a button. David was energetically chopping wood for the fire while I was preparing the food. Everything was late; it had been a long though not arduous day, and it was getting dark. George, as *paterfamilias*, became concerned about David's chopping.

"David, I would be very careful with that axe!"

"Don't worry, George, I know how to use it."

"Well it's late, and the axe is dangerous."

"Christ, George, I'm not a baby! I've used an axe. I'm 41 years old."

"I'm just trying to be safe, " George said. "Since you react in that way, I'm probably right to say something."

David was definitely upset, but after a while the two of them exchanged some quiet words and smoothed the matter over. I never used the axe during the trip. I thought our two Sven saws – triangular saws whose two arms and blade fold up into one length – much safer and easier to use. We all retired to our tents. In our tent Gerd and I exchanged a few words about personalities. Gerd allowed that David, his canoe partner, could be a bit more like the very deliberate and methodical George. Furthermore, the various hazards had impressed themselves on him to such an extent that he declared that he was "concentrating on getting the trip over with safely." He said that George knew what he was doing and that he was going to rely on George and would try not to upset anyone. I thought to myself that Gerd might be too concerned – that, although prudence had to be foremost, worrying too much would prevent him from enjoying the trip.

* * *

On Day 10 we continued down the Cochrane River under a completely overcast sky. From the canoe, the river was not recognizable as a channel

Evening in esker country on the Cochrane.

between clearly defined banks. Its width constantly changed; some wide spots were as much as six miles across. Most of all, the river had so many islands, arms and bays that we could just as well be in a maze of lakes. It was remarkable that George could navigate it. He said that the slight current helped, although it too could sweep into wide bays. The Cochrane is easily discernible on a map, but even then it does not leap out distinctly as a river. It flows northeast from Wollaston Lake and then turns sharply south to empty into Reindeer Lake.

After paddling eleven miles we came to my first honest-to-goodness rapids – Big Stony Rapids. They, for some reason, do not appear on the 1:500,000 map, even though lesser rapids do. In general one cannot rely on rapids being marked on topographical maps. Big Stony looked like a doozy to me: heavy water, with four- or five-foot standing waves in the channel and with turbulent water in two places where waves, reflected from a curving bank and from an island, interfered with those in the channel. We slipped out of the canoes and carefully scouted the rapids from the right bank. My eyes widened and my throat tightened at the sight of the heavy, violent water that extended about three-quarters of a mile. George anticipated no real problems, since there were no rocks or boulders, but we would need to make a couple of moves to avoid the turbulence. We snapped the splash covers on the canoes. This waterproof nylon decking in effect makes them into kayaks. I was sitting in a bow cockpit with the splash cover tied around my waist with a drawstring. George had reviewed beforehand some of the elements of running rapids that I had read about, and now he repeated the basic instructions. I was to respond rapidly as he shouted, from his position of control in the stern, his commands to draw right or left.

We were off. The din of the rapids had been with us even as we had scouted from land; now we hurtled down the middle of the rush and swirl. The noise disappeared from my consciousness as I concentrated on the water and the motion. In no time at all we hit the turbulence. Twice waves thumped me in the chest. And we were through. What a thrill! My first real rapids!

George said that these rapids were of intermediate difficulty – grade three in the vernacular of whitewater canoeists – and that he would consider running them without a splash cover if the canoe were empty and if he were running them for fun nearer to civilization. We continued on, and a mile later we reached another set of grade-three rapids, which were three-quarters of a mile in length. The water was not so heavy, but boulders in the stream called for more manoeuvring. George complimented me on my first whitewater descent. I loved the whole experience. Part of the enjoyment came from having to carefully attend to what we were doing, which required us to be thoroughly engaged in the moment. Very serious consequences could attend a smash-up or a tipping. But it sure was a fast way to go down a river. I may have gushed too much, since George cautioned me about the seriousness of running rapids in the wilderness.

After the rapids we had lunch on a large, flat rock. I made a few casts and caught a five-pound pike. Then Gerd, the most avid fisherman among us, started casting, and an equally large pike nibbled at his lure and followed it to shore a few times. He put down his rod to have a sandwich, whereupon George picked it up and caught the pike.

"See, Gerd, that's how you catch fish."

"Well, could you catch it if I hadn't lured it over here?" Gerd inquired. "You need me to set them up for you."

"Yeah sure, Hartner! A fisherman is the one who catches fish."

George filleted both pikes and put them away for the evening meal.

The overcast turned to rain, and we spent the afternoon paddling through it. We reached Charcoal Lake but did not see the cabins indicated on the map. Eventually we made camp in the rain up a sandy hillside on the west shore of the lake. We were all quite wet from reconnoitering and running the rapids and from the downpour. The steady rain continued, and I thought that we would be in for a miserable camp. But we strung up a tarpaulin, made a big fire at its downwind edge, and warmed up. We watched and salivated as George prepared a fish chowder from the pikes – a pleasant change from the meals prepared from dried mixes. The latter were well planned and tasty, but their consistency and texture were almost always the same – "mush," as Gerd and Dave called them. Everyone did enjoy the excellent chowder under the tarpaulin. The essential ingredient, besides fresh fish, was a pound of canned bacon. George also added dried corn, carrots, spices and, as I was later to learn, what he called his secret ingredient – powdered milk. In fact, I thought that the richness and flavour of the bacon was what exalted the chowder. Each of us had more than a quart of the thick chowder and relished it. We also had instant apple compote for dessert and the ever-present and welcome tea. After a very satisfactory dinner, I smoked my cigar and thought that, despite the afternoon and evening rain, we had had another great day: we had run our first rapids and covered 25 miles.

∗　　∗　　∗

The first thing I did every morning, before leaving the tent, was to stuff my sleeping bag into a nylon bag eighteen inches long and eight inches in diameter. I had to bear down and put my weight on the sleeping bag to get it in and to form a tight cylinder. This morning, as on many others, I had the pleasure of putting on wet socks, wet sneakers and trousers with wet legs. Gerd and I usually hung up socks and underwear on a line that ran under the ridge of our tent, but they did not dry on humid nights. Since we would have to launch canoes after breaking camp and then later might have to jump into the water to beach the canoes or to wrestle them around shallows or rapids, it made no sense to don dry clothes when the day began. Dry clothing was reserved entirely for camp in the evening. Anyway this morning was solidly overcast, and a fine drizzle was still falling.

We had a warm breakfast and continued on Charcoal Lake – a widening of the Cochrane River. To add to the misery, we had to fight a stiff wind. The canoes thumped up and down on the waves. Were it not for the splash covers we would have shipped a lot of water. In fact, it would be impossible to travel on a day like this without the covers. We kept fighting forward. Just as in portaging, there is nothing to do but slog on one step at a time or one stroke at a time. I would not want to spend such a day on the shore anyway. With the normal stroke we made no headway. So I shortened the stroke, reached out, chopped the blade down into the water, and pulled. Reach, chop, grunt – over and over again. I became sullen, began to resent the wind and the lake that were causing me such labour. The chop and the pull on the paddle took on a vicious quality, as if I were striking out at the lake, but we were gaining ground.

The wind diminished mid-lake. We pulled the canoes together and stopped for candy – a custom we followed most days for breaks at mid-morning and -afternoon. From my day bag I gave each person three candies – hard, toffee-like or fruit-filled. We sometimes traded to get our favourites. We had covered six miles in three hours, whereas on a calm day we would have gone eleven.

Soon we were through Charcoal Lake and back on the river proper. We skittered down a riffle and reached Caribou Rapids. We reconnoitered it carefully from the right bank. The rapids were very heavy on the left and in the middle. George picked out a relatively easygoing line near the right side, but we had to avoid a couple of boulders there. The water looked about as violent as that in Big Stony Rapids the previous day, but the extra manoeuvring added a lot of danger. We set out and were swept downstream. George called out to me, "Right, right" or "Left, left," to get around the boulders and avoid being swept down the turbulent centre. His voice was tense. I did reach out fast and pulled hard on the appropriate side. Again, the run was over in no time. We ran the rapids exactly as George had planned. I was very impressed and told him, "George, you seem to know what you are doing."

"It took all I had to keep us on the right hand side of the first boulder," George said.

The other canoe did hit that boulder but luckily avoided any serious mishap. From downstream, George and I watched as Dave and Gerd failed to move the canoe to the right of the boulder. Instead the boulder struck them about three feet from the bow, where Gerd was paddling, and the craft turned sideways to the current – an extremely dangerous situation. The stern, however, was out in the faster central current and spun downstream. The eddy current then swept it behind the boulder, and it turned in behind the boulder. The bow followed. Dave and Gerd had made a complete circle by pivoting around the boulder and ended up facing the right way.

Another set of rapids faced us a little further down the river. Since this one had a shelf entirely across the river, we made a short carry around it on the right. We then ran a third, shorter set without scouting it from shore. George examined it from the calm water at the head by standing up in the canoe. We did scrape over some rocks on the right but with no harm to the sturdy Grumman canoe. George then had us go out towards midstream near the bottom to point out a better route for the other canoe. This brought us within one and a half canoe lengths of some heavy water at the bottom of the rapids. I thought this risky, but George had spotted some large rocks behind which we parked and watched the other canoe descend.

The rain had stopped, but the sky remained overcast. We pushed on, staying close to shore and bumping and scraping rocks now and then. We passed right under a large eagle's nest in a tree overhanging a riffle in the river. Soon we made camp on the east side, in from shore behind some trees and sheltered from the wind. The rapid current had helped us regain time that we had lost against the wind on Charcoal Lake, for we had travelled 28 miles when we made camp at 7:00 p.m. The temperature was 58°F.

Dave and I were cooking again that evening. We made the fireplace, and he gathered wood and started the fire while I prepared the dishes. After cooking and eating I felt querulous, perhaps from being tired and from the dismal weather, and I asked Dave to put some food bags away in the large pack. He evidently did not feel agreeable either – he was about to start washing dishes, and he probably did not enjoy being told what to do, so he replied that the food packs were the cook's job – i.e., mine. I replied that the jobs are not that clearly defined.

57

"The one who perceives the problem should take care of it." Dave said.

I replied, "Yes, I guess that's the way it is. Those are the people who take care of the world. The rest are along for the ride."

This naturally put Dave off, and he said, much to my surprise, "Your bags are light and easy in portages." Then more moderately, "If cooking and washing are unequal we should switch."

"That is probably a good idea," I replied. But the episode was soon over. At the time I thought my comments justified, but on looking back I see that I was causing trouble – I had been reclining against a bag and smoking while ordering Dave around, who had yet to wash the dishes. Dave and I maintained the same roles for the remainder of the trip.

We must have been under a stationary weather front, for the next morning it was still raining. Visibility was poor and navigation among the islands was difficult, but the current helped guide us. Graylings were rising to the surface and taking flies all around us, but we did not bother to break out our rods. We soon reached the northernmost point of the Cochrane River, where it turned sharply south to continue its run towards Reindeer Lake. This turning point is a high prominence where many people had camped or stopped. Shotgun shells, outboard motor oil cans and other junk littered the ground. A forlorn cross, made from a cleft stick with a horizontal piece shoved into it, marked the height. A group had canoed the Cochrane from Wollaston to Reindeer Lake in the early 1970s, and George had the log, kept by Allison Fraser, then about fourteen, who mentioned a child's grave at this place. The dreary weather, the litter and the austere grave all made for a depressing morning.

CHAPTER 8

The Little Lakes

WE LEFT THE COCHRANE AND turned northward up a tributary for one mile. After some difficulty we found the creek, which led to the first of a chain of very small lakes, many of which have no names. George had feared a portage, but the water was high enough and the creeks were clear enough of growth that we could wind our way through them. Reeds were right beside the canoe. Trees overhung us. These confined creeks were friendly and cozy compared to the big waters that we had been travelling. We did haul the canoes twenty yards up and over one small rise. Natives had cut poplar poles and placed them in the water and in the mud of the bank to make it easier to skid their boats up or down. The scars on the bark seemed fresh. I was both disturbed and reassured that we were not the only people to pass this way recently.

As we entered the next lake, we spotted what appeared to be a boulder in the grasses near the opposite shore. When we approached, the boulder became smaller! It was a moose that had turned to present its rump. Soon we could see the splashing as the cow moose immersed its head to feed on the grasses. When its head was under water we paddled closer. When it lifted its head we kept still. In this way we approached to within fifty or sixty yards. We finally disturbed it and, as the moose trotted off through the shallows and into the trees, George captured some fleeting pictures. Unfortunately, the photos did not turn out.

At the next lake – another small one – the sun broke through after two and a half days of solid overcast and rain. We had lunch on top of a high esker overlooking a short connector between two lakes. The wind blew briskly on top. The sun played on islands and water on all sides around us.

59

We were still in the open and varied landscape that marks esker country near the treeline. Clearings of yellow and pale green moss or dark green ground cover, which looked like small blueberry bushes, had taken over the ground between birch and spruce – trees that were like extravagant tufts on a multi-coloured carpet.

After lunch we continued north through a small pond-like lake surrounded by surprisingly large trees and then through a narrow lake 40 yards wide. We then entered a larger, elongated lake bordered by an esker on either side. The sun lit up the landscape from behind us. This far north the sun was not overhead even at noon. The eskers again resembled tended golf courses, covered with swatches of dark green, pale green or yellow, dotted with spruce and birch and interspersed with exposed fine gravel or sand.

We spent the rest of the afternoon hopping from one small lake to another via a number of portages. The portage trails were excellent, well-beaten paths over gravelly eskers used for centuries by Natives, who found the best trails and beat them into the easily scarred soil. Three portages were each a half-mile long. The footing was good, and we had eaten quite a bit of food so the carries were easy. And we were trail hardened. The shorter portages included two consecutive sled-like hauls of the loaded canoes over narrow necks of land.

Finally a narrow channel led us in to the southwest corner of Fort Hall Lake – about five miles long and one mile wide and the largest lake since Charcoal. A trapper's winter cabin, made of plywood sheets and with windows and doors boarded over, overlooked the water. The name Alex Denouygen was written on it. We covered another mile northeast and camped in a clearing near a listing old log cabin.

Dark clouds were returning, but the sun peeped out frequently. The mosquitoes were present in force. A number of them got mixed into the bread dough that I made that evening. After dinner I went to the tent to write my log to the accompaniment of a steady hum. As I looked through the triangular front of the tent I could see a large cloud of mosquitoes on the other side of the net. Later that evening, shortly before sleeping, we heard a wolf howl.

Yet another overcast and drizzly morning greeted us. We rose late and dawdled over breakfast, which featured a novelty – a slice of Canadian back bacon

One of the tents on Fort Hall Lake.

– as well as the more usual grapefruit juice from powder and, as the main course, a quart of oatmeal for each of us, with dried fruit soaked overnight. We added brown sugar, powdered milk, and butter to the oatmeal.

This was to be a day of rest, so we languished in the tents or strolled around and inspected the broken-down cabin until the rain stopped at 10:30. We paddled a few miles to look at the in-flowing Thlewiaza River. Gerd and I fished from a canoe below the rapids near the mouth, while Dave and George hiked up to an esker to look over the countryside. Gerd caught two nice pikes, but I snagged only rocks and lost a lure.

Nobody seems to know where Fort Hall, which gives the lake its name, might have been. P.G. Downes saw no trace of it in 1940. George passed through this lake seven years ago on his way to the Kazan River. We kept an eye out for signs of habitation but did not expect to see anything. A stiff quartering west wind was all the more reason to stop at a promontory – an esker on the east side overlooking the sandy narrows. There, clustered together on the hill, were four burial sites, each surrounded by a fence made of white pickets two feet high. Each had a cross inside. Two of the enclosures were so small that they could have contained only infants. Some of the fences were completely down, probably from snowstorms or animals. Separate from the four a prominent gravesite overlooked the lake. George said that the last time he was through it had contained a cross on which the name Kasmere had been cut. We located no cross with the name, but we did find one with the date 1940. Kasmere was an influential and effective Chipewyan leader in this area from just before 1900, when J.B. Tyrrell, the Canadian explorer, met him.

In *Sleeping Island*, P.G. Downes describes meeting Kasmere in 1939: "As we left the canoe and went up to meet them, the talk died down. We were met by a ring of dark faces, black, staring eyes, and complete silence. In the center of the group was one very old man, still broad, squat, and powerful looking. He was wearing a ten-pound flour sack sewed together into a hood with a high peak. It gave him an odd gnomish look. I recognized him immediately. It was old Kasmere. Next to him was another old man who looked for all the world like an apparition out of a child's fairy tale. He had a big beaked nose and craggy eyebrows, and upturned chin, and black beady eyes. Him I recognized also. It was Edzanni ("Gull-droppings"), reputed to be a great rascal. These two older men seemed to dominate the group, and I went straight to them, shook hands, and called them each by name. They immediately broke out into voluble, guttural Chipewyan, simultaneously streaming through the worn brown teeth of both so that it was impossible to make out a single word. The others of the group but one were much younger men." The Chipewyan had travelled back and forth between Reindeer Lake and the barren lands for centuries. They had established the portage trails, which we used, but their descendants now lived in coastal villages or in settlements on some of the larger lakes, leaving the interior basically deserted. I wished that we had encountered indigenous people in the way they lived before everything changed.

We had lunch and decided to wait out the wind. We were in no hurry – we had plenty of food and only five more days of travel would take us to Nueltin Lake, where we would resupply. Each of us went off by himself – Gerd to read and to write his diary, Dave and George to sleep and explore.

I took my sneakers off in an attempt to dry them and my socks in the wind and then lay down in a moss clearing and dozed, using my lifejacket as a pillow. In our existence, small bits of comfort took on unusual importance, and I went to some effort to achieve them. I wanted to lie in the sun, but in the lee there were too many mosquitoes, and on completely exposed parts of the esker the wind was too strong. When some sprinkles of rain began to fall, I crawled under a small spruce, taking my lifejacket and diary with me. As I did on most days, I was wearing my Gore-Tex jacket. When the hood was up and drawn tight, my face was exposed only from eyebrows to nose. What with wearing glasses, I could hunker down comfortably with the few mosquitoes on top of the esker. I felt like an animal – dozing on the moss, snuggled under a tree – and quite at ease, feeling comfortable with my immediate circumstances but also because I felt so at one with the place.

When I had my fill of snoozing, I wrote in my diary, still lolling on the moss. The sky was a play of contrasts as bright sun came out now and then from between large dark clouds.

✶   ✶   ✶

The purpose of the diary, one would think, was – what else? – to record events and impressions so that we could recall them later, making the trip live longer. But the diary came to serve another purpose too. It was the only way to keep track of dates and days filled with the tasks of existence – days pretty much the same and tasks that were essential, about which we had no option but to do them, to paddle onward, to cook, eat, sleep, and then do it again. The diary ordered life and tied it to a calendar, to a scheme that perhaps made some sense apart from mere existence, especially since as we updated our diaries we traced out our path on a map, noting lunch and camp sites and dates. So our journey, which on the water and on the eskers seemed like endless, repetitive wandering, on the map looked to be progress – a sinuous, but seemingly orderly line connecting places and dates.

Perhaps retaining this connection to calendar and dates prevented total immersion in this – for us – new world. And leaving maps at home would have rendered us more intimately part of that world. Lack of reference to anything outside our immediate surroundings would have allowed us to

Dave at the falls of the Thlewiaza River, near Fort Hall Lake.

experience them more deeply. We would have had to discover for ourselves and by ourselves what was around the bend or up the river, rather than anticipating it with the aid of cartographers. But I did not think, let alone utter, such a thought until the trip was over.

So each of us kept a diary, quite faithfully, but as far as I know none of us shared or was asked to share what we entered there, at that time. (Afterwards George did send me a typed version of his matter-of-fact log.) Everyone wrote in his logbook. Perhaps we wrote for loved ones back home. Perhaps we wanted to retain connections, to remind ourselves that a world of creature comforts – of jobs and responsibilities, of newspapers, music and art – existed and that we were a part of it. Perhaps we wanted to remember that we were creatures of other than the wilderness. For a variety of unarticulated reasons, I felt quite a strong compunction to maintain my log. We all kept diaries and wrote in them regularly.

✶   ✶   ✶

Eventually an animal will rise from its rest and go on the prowl, or simply go for a walk, and that is what I did that lazy afternoon when the sun broke through for a longer period, although the black clouds were still all about. I strolled for an hour among the spruce, sauntering on the moss and savouring life on solid ground.

At 5:00 p.m. the wind died down, so we paddled five miles and then made camp on the western shore of Thanout Lake. The sun was out for the most part, but so were the large clouds. We had a pleasant campsite on a sandy and grassy point. I cooked vegetable and barley soup, macaroni and cheese with mung beans from the dried mixes, and a side dish of Gerd's fish, dipped in batter and fried. And of course there was dessert – raisins and walnut bits in hot lemon sauce. Frying the fish took more care than cooking mush. It was quite a lot of work, but the result was a tasty and, as usual, gargantuan meal, which marked the end of a relaxing day.

✶   ✶   ✶

The next day we explored an old trading post at the north end of Thanout Lake. It was well-built and sturdy. Wooden pegs held the logs together, but nails and tarpaper had also been used. Logs nearby marked the site of a collapsed cabin. Tyrell had visited Chief Red Hair here in 1894, per-

66

haps in the old cabin. Several markers – buildings, grave sites of the previous day and of the coming evening at the eastern arm of Kasmere Lake,
and well-beaten portage trails – clearly indicated a major thoroughfare
used by the Chipewyan between the Cochrane River and Nueltin Lake.
Their descendants do not travel the waterways much now, preferring to
stay near government posts.

We followed the Thlewiaza River northeastward and reached a portage
of over a mile, which took us around Kasmere Falls. The trail was again
a clear path, but the portage did take us up and down hills and through
some mud in low spots. It was well inland, away from the water, and rather
easy, in great contrast to our labours on the way to Wollaston Lake.

The day continued sunny as we entered the shimmering expanse of Kasmere Lake, very different from Fort Hall and Thanout Lakes, which are
just stretches where the Thlewiaza River widens to as much as a mile. The
prospect of a bright day on open water was pleasant. We had last experienced it five days earlier on entering the Cochrane. Spending every minute
of every day outdoors during these two weeks had made me very con-
scious of the sky and of the play of light under various cloud conditions
and at different times of the day. The midday sun on Kasmere Lake was
stark but not hot. On the distant shore we spotted regular shapes of orange
and blue – a sign of humans pleasing for its novelty but a violation of our
pristine wilderness. As we approached the beach on the southern tip of
the large point around which the two major arms of Kasmere Lake extend,
we saw a number of tents and some forty oil drums. No one was in the
camp, but the gear bore the Canadian Fisheries Department label. The
tents were closed up. Coolers for meat and vegetables were dug into the
sand of the beach. Presumably the people were dispersed for their day's
work. We took advantage of the sunny day and the beach to bathe and
wash underwear, which later dried easily on top of our packs in the canoes.
Then we continued northeastward. Some clouds came out and scattered
showers fell, but the day for the most part was ideal for canoeing.

CHAPTER 9

Finns and Reflections

AS WE DESCENDED A RIFFLE where the Thlewiaza River leaves Kas mere Lake, I was startled to see two people fishing from an aluminum canoe – the first humans since Wollaston Post and the first that we had seen on the water. They wore felt fedoras, slickers and rubber boots. We hailed them and pulled our canoes beside theirs. They were brothers who had left Reindeer Lake eighteen days earlier and had travelled up the Cochrane. In other words, they had started in the same place as we did, but we had looped to the east and north to Wollaston Lake. Even more surprising, they were Finns living in Sweden who wanted to spend their vacation in the Canadian wilderness. One of them spoke good English, while the other just smiled. They said that two others from Sweden had been along but "got bored or something" and had turned back a week into the trip.

We inquired about their supplies and were assured that they had ample. They did ask for sweets or cookies and for bread when they found that we baked. I gave them about a pound and a half of candy. George dug out one of our dinners and a couple of pounds of sugar as well as a loaf of bread and handed them over. They started on the candies eagerly. After chatting for half an hour, we left them to their grayling fishing and paddled on.

We made camp on the right bank of the Thlewiaza a couple of miles further downstream. When the Finns paddled into sight we waved them over and they joined us, pitching their small canvas tent close to water's edge. All of us looked forward to enlarging our society for an evening, particularly with other canoeists. Penti, the senior of the two by a couple of years, and probably no older than thirty, was the leader and spokesman, presumably because his English was better. He was a slim blond whose laconic manner conveyed competence. When asked if he was an expert canoeist in the rapids, he quietly replied, "Well, not expert precisely, but I have done a lot of whitewater canoeing." His brother Matti, who had no beard stubble and only a trace of a moustache, seemed so androgynous that at first I thought that he might be female. Matti hardly spoke but seemed to understand what was said, since he laughed at the right moments.

We cooked one of our dinners. The proportions were about right to feed the six of us, and our guests enjoyed it. They relished the tea; perhaps they had none of their own. After dinner Dave passed around his rum, and then Matti reciprocated with some Dutch brandy. Penti earned his living by making orienteering maps – which suggests the extent of that sport in the Nordic countries. The two were on this trip to northern Canada because there are few undammed rivers in their part of the world and they wanted to get away from people.

Penti was clearly an experienced canoeist and outdoorsman. When asked how he finds portage trails, some of which are obscure in the extreme, he said that he looks very carefully or climbs a nearby hill – although the Nunavut landscape does not have many prominent ones. I thought it quite a feat for them to travel such a distance to make a long wilderness trip that very few Canadians attempt. Penti did say that the climate, landscape and conditions in general were similar to those in northern Norway, Sweden and Finland.

They seemed to be impressed with our gear and our organization and remarked on them. We *were* much better equipped than they. Their tent and clothing appeared to be of heavy cotton. They wore rubberized rain gear. We, in contrast, had modern fabrics: nylon tents and Gore-Tex or nylon rain gear.

Most of all, our food and cooking arrangements differed. They said that they ate a lot of rice, beans, lentils, and fish, while our food, other than lunches, was a dried mix for a variety of courses.

The contrast made me see how well our system was working. George had organized everything – equipment, food and duty rosters – in an almost military manner. We ate three different breakfasts throughout the trip, each served with brown sugar and milk made from powder. We boiled either oatmeal or Red River cereal (a mixture of grains) and then mixed it with dried fruit that had been allowed to soak overnight. Every third

Gerd and Dave on the Thlewiaza River.

morning we had a cold granola cereal. Each person ate at least a full quart of cereal every morning. We also had orange or grapefruit juice made from powder. As a special treat we sometimes had a piece of Canadian bacon. Before the trip nobody had insisted on coffee, so we had none along, but some mornings we did make tea. I had been used to light breakfasts in the city, but on the trip I quickly grew to appreciate a hearty breakfast.

Our dinners were varied and consisted of a number of courses. The menu was elaborate and would have done a fine restaurant proud. While the listing of meals and courses sounded elegant, we made everything from freeze-dried mixes. Nevertheless, David and Denise had planned, organized and packed them so that we had a great variety of interesting meals easily accessible and available. George said that he had not experienced anything like it on any of his trips.

For example, the six dinner menus (including preparation times and total weights) for the first and third weeks were as follows (the seventh dinner of the week we improvised – for example, by cooking fish that we had caught):

SUPPERS IN WEEKS 1 AND 3

Supper No. 1

Cream of Chicken Soup	10 min.
Italian Noodles	15 min.
Rice Pudding and Caramel Sauce	10 min.
4 lb. 4 oz.	

Supper No. 2

Lentil Soup	45 min.
Seasoned Rice	25 min.
Stroganoff Noodles	20 min.
Tapioca Fruit Pudding	20 min.
4 lb. 1 oz.	

Supper No. 3

Mushroom-Potato Soup	15 min.
Fusili in Tomato and Cheese Sauce	30 min.
Creamed Carrots	15 min.
Apricot Cream Rice	20 min.
4 lb. 4 oz.	

Supper No. 4

Barley and Vegetable Soup	15 min.
Macaroni and Cheese	25 min.
Nut and Seed Patties with Apple Sauce	15 min.
Raisin Lemon Sauce	20 min.
4 lb. 6 oz.	

Supper No. 5

Cornmeal Cheese Soup	25 min.
Chili Kidney Beans	50 min.
Blueberry Pudding Cake	20 min.
4 lb. 2 oz.	

Supper No. 6

Pea Soup	15 min.
Millet Goulash	30 min.
Date Squares	5 min.
Chocolate Pudding	
3 lb. 4 oz.	

Our bread mix was packed one loaf per plastic bag. The reflector oven for baking folded up flat. Our cooking grate was also very compact – two stainless steel pipes each two feet long. Each of our four cooking pots sat within the next larger one, and the smallest one contained the six quart-sized, deep plastic bowls from four of which we ate. These bowls rarely got rinsed between courses of a dinner.

Our chores and duties were also organized. Each of us canoed with one person, tented with another, and did camp chores with the third. Two people cooked and washed dishes, while the other two put up and took down our two tents; the next day these duties would be switched.

The pair cooking and washing dishes divided their responsibilities as they saw fit. Fixed roles rapidly emerged, but some swapping of duties did take place. For example, when David and I cooked, Dave usually got up first and started the fire. I then cooked the Red River cereal or oatmeal, and in rare instances bacon, and mixed the milk powder and the juice. The milk went in the cereal, as did the dried fruit mixture that the cook of that day soaked overnight. Dave would then wash the breakfast dishes, and I would place the cups and cutlery bag into the small back-pack that we call our lunch bag.

A lunch stop required only unpacking the lunch bag and Dave's kettle. All the large bags stayed undisturbed in the canoes. The cook in the twosome then cut up the loaf of bread into twelve slices and mixed either iced tea or lemonade in the kettle. I also cut up cheese or salami most days, but the bulk of the meal consisted of bread spread copiously with peanut butter, jam, butter or frequently all three.

For supper in the next camp Dave and I would prepare a fireplace out of rocks, preferably three large ones – one to reflect heat from the back and two at the sides to support the pipes. Then while Dave gathered wood and started the fire, I measured cups of water into the pots, stirred and so on. About every second night we baked bread before any cooking – it took a while and we usually needed, for cooking, the large pot in which we kneaded the bread mix (with three cups of water and one-third of a cup of corn oil). I usually baked the bread, but Dave tried it a couple of times. Then, after the meal, Dave would wash the dishes. I usually filled the used pots with water and put them back on the fire to get warm water for dishwashing.

Gerd and George would have an easier time that evening, only putting up the tents. However, after dinner George made sure that the bread, cups and cutlery were in the lunch bag for the next day and prepared the dried fruit for soaking overnight. George was the cook on his team, and Gerd gathered firewood and washed dishes. The next morning George and Gerd did the breakfast, while Dave and I took down the tent.

Such regimentation may seem peculiar for a summer jaunt in canoes, but in fact we were on a wilderness expedition with significant dangers. George had developed the system from his extensive experience. Life was simpler and safer, since our duties were clear, bickering about chores was minimized, and we knew where to find things. Although we had worked hard to omit unnecessary gear, we still had six large bags and, for each of us, small personal bags, with everything compactly packed away, so finding an item might be difficult. The few times I had to dig around – for example, to find a nail clipper after breaking a nail – really made me appreciate the system. George also told us about some of his early trips when people had to rummage in many packs to get each meal together.

The advantages and disadvantages of an organized state held true in our micro-society. Freedom and responsibility intertwined. Though the regimentation might seem restrictive – you could not do whatever you wanted to at any given time because the others depended on you to do your job – you did not have to worry about every need because you knew that the others were doing their jobs and that these needs would be met. In fact, in the evening the pair not cooking and washing up had lots of time to write logs, photograph or wander about and do nothing.

We did take time out to rest, go hiking or just dawdle around, but usually only when high winds forced us to do so and only occasionally because the opportunity was attractive. When we faced open water and favourable weather – quite common that summer – we pressed on. Our equipment and organization had allowed us to not only make up a head start of a week that the Finns had, but to also travel over a longer and more difficult route. The Finns, however, probably enjoyed the time that they spent fishing for a significant fraction of their food. Our rate of progress, however, was nothing like that of the voyageurs of the fur trade. At any rate, George had developed the system, and we followed it with only mild comments about fascism.

✶ ✶ ✶

The others were sleeping late the next day when I rousted them out at 7:30. We breakfasted and, as we were leaving, I saw another contrast between the Finns and us: they were baking a grayling by holding it over a fire with a forked stick. At least they would not have to wash a cooking pan.

We ran a couple of rapids before reaching Sucker Lake. The Thlewiaza River is powerful here. Our splash covers were on, and a good thing too. The bow dug into standing waves a couple of times, and I got smashed in the chest and slapped in the face by water. I gripped the paddle tightly, even desperately. The collisions with the waves sent enough water past the drawstring of the decking around my waist to soak my trousers and feet thoroughly, but we passed through in fine shape. I again found it exhilarating. Then we made short work of the seven miles of Sucker Lake and, upon emerging, had still more fun running a modest set of rapids. I thought that the last three days encapsulated the wonderful variety of our trip – canoeing on narrow Thanout Lake and the Thlewiaza River, portaging, rapids, flat open water on Kasmere Lake, and a diversity of campsites.

We climbed a high, steep esker carrying our lunch. At 120 feet high, this esker provided the best overview yet of the surrounding countryside. The green of the ever-present spruce forest, dotted with ponds, lakes and streams, stretched out below in all directions. The winding Thlewiaza offered the only semblance of regularity. A light green bowl nearby, about an acre in size, had once been a pond but was now filled with reeds and muck and was on its way to becoming completely filled.

A chilling wind made me welcome my Gore-Tex jacket and lifejacket vest, but it did dry out our trousers and shoes. Who would have thought that a lifejacket would be useful on a hilltop? The wind did not chase away the blackflies, which were out in abundance, but it did keep them in our lee. We faced into the wind, just as the caribou do, while we ate lunch. The blackflies peppered the back of my hood. Then we took a short walk along the esker to enjoy the view, but the combination of cool wind and blackflies was not inviting.

After lunch our canoes entered a long, wide, shallow rapids. They bumped from rock to rock and grated over others. We were almost sledding down these waters – possible in our aluminum Grumman canoe, generally considered a tough, forgiving workhorse. Aficionados debate at length the merits of materials, styles and manufacturers best suited for different types of canoeing. The Grummans, though somewhat lumbering and heavy, are considered almost indestructible. They continue to be used for wilderness trips because repairs are rarely necessary, although various modern plastic or Kevlar canoes are increasingly in favour. The Grummans have served George well over the years. We lived in them and relied on them, and I became fond, very fond, of ours, as I would of any item on which my life depended.

Later we came to a more respectable rapid, marked as a "falls" on the map. We carried our craft along a large, flat shelf of granite and put it back in below the worst stretch. The river continued shallow and rocky, so we had to jump out and haul the canoe over some stretches, line it a little, or just scrape along. All this was around a sharp southward bend in the river. It might have been easier to portage across the point of land.

Camp was in the trees at the bottom of the set of rapids. The evening sun shone brightly as we consumed a pleasant and, as usual, too large a meal. A brief shower sprinkled us during dessert but soon ended. The Thlewiaza runs west to east there, and the sun's intense horizontal evening light soon sparkled off the chuckling current and caused the green shore on the other side to glow softly.

We expected to resupply the next day at Nueltin Lake. The first portion of the trip was coming to an end. This was our fifteenth camp. After dinner, as I relaxed and gazed over the river to the other shore, I reflected on the easy day just winding down, on the pleasant setting, and on the approach of our resupply, which would bring some contact with the rest of the world. A sense of wellness suffused my being.

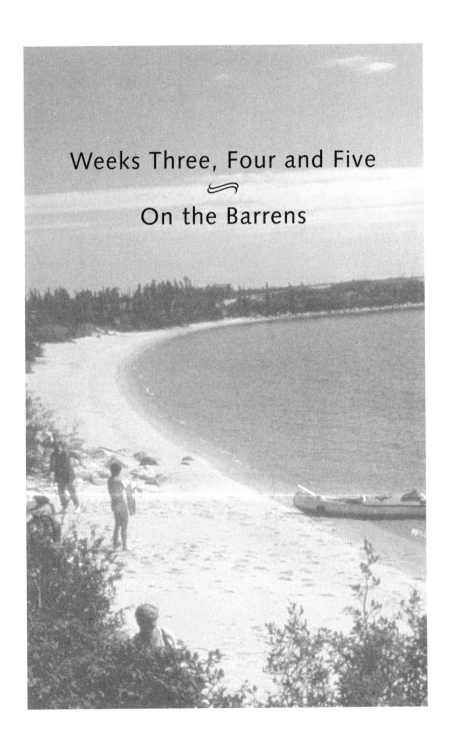

Weeks Three, Four and Five

On the Barrens

CHAPTER 10

Sleeping Island and Resupply

W E STARTED EACH DAY WITH chores: stuffing the sleeping bag into its container bag with fingers that were stiff, claw-like, from grasping the paddle all the previous day, then making breakfast or breaking the tent and loading the canoe. Each morning also brought anticipation of what we would see and experience that day. It began with a glance at the weather, which was ever-present in a way that a city dweller cannot imagine. It was like another person along with us on the trip – a domineering character whose influence we could not escape, no matter what we happened to be doing.

Each day was much like any other in overall structure – get up, travel, have lunch, travel, make camp and sleep. But the details of each were novel. We were travelling through country that we had never seen. What would be around the next bend? How would this particular combination of wind and temperature affect us? How did the sun play on the clouds and on the water? We were so essentially connected to our surroundings and to what we were doing that we felt exhilaration even when the particular task might be the grinding drudgery of paddling against a stiff wind or gasping and stumbling across a rough portage.

Everything that we did – each carry, each meal, each paddle stroke – was necessary for us to continue, to survive and to return home. Life was simple and immediate; the distractions and convolutions that bedevil and enrich civilization receded into dim memory, leaving us alive in the moment. Are such romantic reflections possible in retrospect only because the memory of constantly wet feet and swarms of blackflies has vanished? Yes, the unpleasant experiences do diminish in hindsight, but so does the stark thrill of being vitally linked to one's surroundings. Fortunately, the pleasant recollections fade less than the unpleasant ones. Memories are fine, but being there is better.

✶   ✶   ✶

This day would be different. After fifteen days in the wilderness we would encounter an outpost of civilization at Treeline Lodge, a fly-in fishing camp where our supplies for the remainder of the trip were waiting. First we had to make a run of twelve or fifteen miles into the southwestern corner of Nueltin Lake, which the Chipewyan had called Sleeping Island Lake.

As we took a channel of the Thlewiaza River that arched north of the shallow, reedy Sandy Lake, we came upon a bull moose feeding in the shallows. We approached it while its head was immersed in the water; then we remained still when it lifted its head, and resumed paddling towards it when it lowered its head again. When we were within 50 yards, it looked at us curiously, almost disdainfully, and then trotted off into the woods. We continued down the Thlewiaza, entered Nahili Lake and crossed its southern portion with a quick pull of four miles.

Before we entered Nueltin Lake we had to run a couple of rapids. They looked serious, but we were close to our new supplies – the horses could smell the barn. We examined the rapids briefly and then ran the route exactly as George had called, but not without some vigorous paddling. George called out from the stern, "go left, left! LEFT!" and I leaned out far on the left side, placed most of my weight on the paddle, and drew it straight in towards the canoe once, twice and a third time, and we avoided the rock. (The action of the draw stroke can change the canoe's direction and momentarily stabilize it by bracing it against the flow. The extended paddle and draw inward produce an outrigger effect.)

Soon we saw boats and a few buildings on the beach to the left of us in the small bay into which the Thlewiaza enters the lake. As we paddled up, we saw a middle-aged guest and his son of about twenty getting out of a motorboat at the dock. A Native guide took the boat to the dock and tied it up and held it so that the people could climb out. The customers wore heavy coats. We learned later that they had flown in the previous day from Chicago via Winnipeg. It was mainly sunny and about 50°F – a normal July day near the Manitoba/Northwest Territories border. We, in the canoes, were tanned, unshaven and in shirts. The guests glanced at us curiously and barely nodded.

After two weeks of living, eating, sleeping and working entirely out-doors, we found contact a bit disconcerting, even alienating. I could not help but feel distant from those people at the lodge. They might have appropriate dress for zipping along in a motorboat, but we were outfit-ted to make our way with our own efforts, toiling with paddles. We had taken fifteen days to reach the lodge; they, a couple of hours to fly twice that distance from Winnipeg. I was certain that I derived more pleasure from the journey than they. But in my smugness and self-satisfaction I did allow that they too could be enjoying themselves.

We landed and quickly retrieved the cardboard cartons of our food. The formidable pile looked impossible to cram into only two canoes. But a canoeist is an efficient packer. By now we all had done lots of packing and, with some effort, we placed everything into our canvas packs in a couple of hours, tightly and densely jammed together.

We chatted with lodge owner Bill Bennett, a couple of his guides, and two guests in the small lobby of the main building. The place was heated with a Franklin stove; after a while the warmth and, I thought, stuffiness became oppressive, and I urged the others to leave. I wanted to be out in the open air, with no artificial heat, where the breezes could play on us. The others did point out that mosquitoes and blackflies could also prey on us.

Bill Bennett, in his early or mid-thirties, spent the summer at the lodge with his wife and son, then about four. He ran an efficient and well-organ-ized operation. At least one of his customers agreed with that impression, and his guides liked the place too, since they had work all summer – the lodge was booked solid.

The encounter with civilized life also stimulated me to think about my family and allowed me to send a letter to them. I wrote it; one of the fish-ermen took it south with him and posted it in Chicago; it arrived in Florida in about ten days.

*   *   *

Since we had made excellent time, George was planning a forty- or fifty-mile excursion from our original route. He wanted to veer slightly east of Nueltin Lake and visit Windy River and Windy Lake, which would

80

Heading overland from Nueltin Lake towards Windy Lake

avoid some of the large expanses of open water in the northern half of Nueltin and permit us to see an abandoned trading post on Windy River. One of Bennett's guides, who had trapped in the Windy River area and still does each winter, answered questions about portages and rapids on the proposed route.

George gave Bennett a copy of P.G. Downes' *Sleeping Island*. The book contains pictures of the Natives whom the author encountered at Nueltin Lake and on the Cochrane River in 1939. When we passed through, 42 years after Downes had, the Native guides were delighted to recognize some of their relatives in the photos. The guides stood around quietly in the lodge, watching and waiting, as we transacted the business with Bennett. They were friendly and helpful when we approached them and asked about the routes between the lakes and about their travels. They were wiry and five feet eight inches tall at most – small compared to the four of us.

Bennett's mechanic, Al, was loquacious and ready with off-colour quips. He suggested a spot where we might camp that evening after we left the lodge. Al had a Native wife and at least one child. Their winter home was in Red Lake – a mining town in northern Ontario, considerably south of our current location. Al told us how the fishing camp went up and about how the builders landed a DC-3 and constructed a ramp from large logs cut near by so that they could unload a bulldozer, which they used to construct a gravel airstrip.

The day at the lodge was pleasant for its novelty, but I was pleased to be off in the canoes again and glad to make camp in the open air a few miles later. Most of our resupply consisted of our usual freeze-dried mixtures, but we had also purchased some fresh food for a celebratory meal that night. We had steaks, fresh potatoes and onions, beer and wine, and some fresh cherries. We fixed the meat, potatoes and onions. The large steaks curled up the steep sides of our two-quart plastic bowls – the one and only set of dishes that we used. Our usual meals never required cutting, so now we made do with our Swiss army or hunting knives, whatever each of us had. I decided to simply cut the steak in half and take bites from it while holding it in my fingers – and I was not the only one to adopt these table manners. We savoured the fresh fixings. We rested on the flat rocks above a small sandy beach as we chatted and sipped our beverages. The few mosquitoes were hardly noticeable. A colourful sunset through a partly cloudy sky, together with the fine meal and the beer and wine – and the satisfaction of a speedy first half of the trip and resupply in good order – brought enormous contentment, even pride.

The upbeat feeling continued on the following morning, clear and sunny, but during the day a slight queasiness came over me. I realized that I might be hungover. I had drunk two bottles of beer and a third of a bottle of wine during our feast. (Gerd does not touch wine, so he had more beer.) This relatively modest amount was enough to discombobulate my system after two weeks of wholesome, vigorous living. Vegetarians might blame the pound of fresh beef.

Perhaps I was not the only one feeling out of sorts. We never left trash at a campsite – always burned or buried everything. But the previous night we had beer and wine bottles, and that day George said, "Let's see, Gerd. I guess you got rid of the bottles in the lake. I did not see you do it."

Gerd: "Well, I had to work at it – to stopper them up!"

"Stopper them up?" George asked.

I chuckled, and Gerd replied, "Yeah, otherwise they would sink when I put them in the lake. Jesus Christ, George! You're like a mother without tits."

The day got warmer as we paddled on and on. Digging the paddle into the water became a chore. The south end of Nueltin Lake is a maze of islands, and in my lassitude the variety of them took on a dreary sameness. George did a fine job of navigating us through them. At lunch everyone took advantage of the warm day to jump in the chilly lake for a quick bath and a wash of underwear. Nobody dallied too long in the sunlight and slight breeze because there were bugs out. We slipped back into our outer clothes and, as before, left the underwear on top of the packs in the canoes to dry in the sun.

The late afternoon brought some relief from the sun in the form of clouds and light showers. The islands that we passed signalled the approach of the barren lands. Some of them had very few trees, and those that we did see were short and stunted, sprouting here and there amid the moss and bare gravel and boulders. We were at the treeline. And sometime that afternoon we crossed from Manitoba into the Northwest Territories – into what is now Nunavut.

We paddled almost 32 miles that day and made camp on the west side of Nueltin Lake, just south of a thick swatch of islands where the waist of the lake begins. This camp brought our first really serious exposure to black-flies. Thick clouds of them were everywhere. We had on rain jackets with hoods up. The flies sounded like rain as they peppered the hood. They seemed to love dark wool, as a squirming sheet of bugs covered my pant legs. I slathered my hands with bug lotion to prepare to cook dinner. Everyone put head nets on for the first time but had to remove them for the meal, so we ate fast and hurried back into the nets or into the tents. George went for a walk wearing his bug jacket, made of light, coarse netting impregnated with bug juice – insect repellent. From inside the tent we heard the blackflies spattering the nylon and saw them hovering in malevolent clouds outside the netting of the entrance. The ones that did penetrate the tent wanted out and concentrated at the opening inside the entrance net, where we could easily kill them. I rushed into the tent and wrote in my trip log. I wondered what the repellent was doing to my skin, because at 95 per cent

Sunny day on a fine beach – a perfect opportunity for a bath.

DEET – the strongest available – it softened the plastic of my ballpoint pen. I also hoped that I would not have to pee in the night, because I did not want to go outside. From that day on, I always carried my head net and a small bottle of bug repellent in my jacket pockets. These items joined another essential – a small roll of toilet paper. The bugs were not too bad first thing in the morning, but they soon appeared in force. The one sure relief was to move out onto the water and paddle away from shore. They generally cannot keep up with the moving canoe, and there is usually some breeze out on the water, although occasionally blackflies do hitch a ride a long way out by drafting in the lee behind a paddler.

✳   ✳   ✳

A hill 300 feet high is a prominent landmark in these parts and after breakfast we set out for the one nearby and hiked up a gentle incline across rocks, grass and a few shrubs. After a couple of miles of walking along this tundra we reached the top, where a breeze kept away the blackflies that had annoyed us on the way up, particularly when we had passed through hollows and in the lee of large boulders. The view from the top offered our first perspective of the countryside from any elevation of significance. Blotches of water and land stretched out in all directions, with some enormous expanses of water to the east showing Nueltin Lake and Hearne Bay. The dappled land – brown rocks and shades of green from grasses, mosses, shrubs and occasional treed areas – was matched by a large blue sky, with clouds to the south and darker thunder clouds to the northwest, from some of which fell a drapery of rain.

No sign of people in any direction, until we looked down and saw the outline of a human figure laid out with cantaloupe-size stones on a large flat rock. This hilltop is a natural feature that would attract travellers, as it had drawn us, and evidently at least one other group.

Gerd, managing lunch that day, received some gibes for having laid out the fixings in the lee of some six-foot-high boulders. We praised him for arranging a kitchen that featured its own host of blackflies. We made our sandwiches and scurried back into the stiff wind to eat facing the breeze. If you turned too quickly, you walked into the flies lurking in your lee.

Peter, Dave, George and Gerd, relatively clean after bathing, pose for a group portrait.

Are these blackflies inside or outside the tent?

After returning to camp, we made a short paddle and then began a mile-long portage north towards Windy Lake. We bushwhacked – headed across country without benefit of any established trail. The going was rough over jumbled rocks, with brush clutching at our calves and knees. Our enormous loads made the carry even more difficult. Not only had we just received a three-and-a-half week food supply, but it was also an unusually heavy one. We had planned a week of flat-water paddling along the immense Nueltin Lake, with no portaging, so we had brought canned food rather than the much lighter freeze-dried stuff. But our fast progress allowed an excursion westward to Windy River and Windy Lake across some portages. Now we were being punished for our hard work and fortunate weather; now each can of ham or chicken made its presence felt as we staggered across the portage.

After a short paddle across a half-mile pond we again had to portage. This time after labouring up a very steep esker we arrived at clear ground; everyone was relieved and ready to make camp. For supper we had a mod-

86

est reward of canned lobster bisque, undercooked beans – they just take too long to cook, I claimed – and chocolate pudding.

Dozens of narrow trails laced the area, worn into the sand and gravel. They crossed occasionally but generally tended northward along the dry, high ground. We were following the path of the caribou – a track that they had probably used for years. After dinner I hiked along it to yet higher ground to catch a better breeze and to enjoy the sunset, a cup of tea and a Cuban cigar – my real reward. As I basked in the serenity of the purpling sky and the gently undulating countryside, the day's exertions receded, and I again felt at peace with this isolated land – a tranquility perhaps earned on the portage and through coexistence with the blackflies.

✶   ✶   ✶

The morning of Day 18 was ideal for paddling – cool, with scattered clouds, a mild breeze and no bugs once we were a reasonable distance from shore. We had ascended a bit from Nueltin Lake and the land was now quite flat. We were on an immense sheet of water with occasional islands and peninsulas adding some variety, and with a parallel sheet of sky above us also interspersed with its own islands of clouds. A portage, well marked and worn smooth, took us into Windy Lake. Later, the day became cloudless and warmer and eventually too warm for perfectly comfortable paddling. Lunch was on top of one esker, and our evening camp was on another. In both places the utter solitude of the islands, green with ground cover and large expanses of water under a bright sky, made me think that there was nowhere else that I would then rather be.

I used the early stop and the fine weather for a quick bath and wash of underwear, while the others did sewing repairs and George strengthened his seat in the canoe, the aluminum of which had cracked. The water was cool and the sun was warm, but I did not tarry naked in either the water or in the sun, since the bugs were out and the breeze was too mild to keep them at bay. I dried off in a rush and raced back into my clothes. It is too bad that blackflies are interested in warm-blooded animals. George said that they subsist on some kind of vegetable matter when people are not around.

"They should stick to their regular diet." I said.

To which Gerd commented, "Their regular diet is like eating freeze-dried mush, but when we come around it's like having salami."

I made bread and cooked dinner (1.5 pounds of canned ham, mashed potatoes, fried sesame seeds and syrup). We were in head nets most of the time. I soon retired to the tent to write in my log, look through the screen and the cloud of flies hovering there, and watch the sun set in the northwest. The soft light, rich and golden, darkened over the green esker and the calm lake. The bugs do get in everywhere. Gerd and I had bloody ankles and calves, despite rolling our socks up over the pant legs and fastening them with rubber bands. I had a line of welts along my back around the belt line from exposure when I bent over and my shirt pulled out. They itched much less than mosquito bites but, with their centre of dark, congealed blood surrounded by a red, inflamed circle a half-inch in diameter, they surely appeared scrofulous.

At 7:30 the next morning, after breaking camp with the by-now-familiar stiff fingers – my hands cramped and claw-like, even after a relatively short paddling day – we were out on the water. We followed a channel of the Windy River and then went a mile up the Red River to an old Hudson's Bay Company post that author P.G. Downes had been so happy to reach. It had marked the culmination of his journey and the place where he got to know the Natives. Two cabins still stood, or at least kneeled, but were on their way down. A couple of miles downstream, at the south end of Simons Lake, sits another cabin, which one of the guides at Bill Bennett's lodge uses as a winter trappers' cabin.

We enjoyed a superb day paddling in the area that marked fulfillment of at least one goal of our trip – to retrace Downes' journey. We had now done that and were about halfway into our trip. The forty or fifty feet of elevation that we had gained by portaging into Windy Lake descended smoothly back into Nueltin Lake over about ten or twelve miles. Occasionally there was a fast current and we could – with a stretch of the imagination – have called a couple of places rapids, although the map did not mark them as such. They did perk us up on that warm, almost sultry afternoon. Where the Windy River empties into Smith Bay – a large arm that extends about fifteen miles northwestward from Nueltin Lake – we came on yet another old cabin. This one had the remnants of a tower-like structure attached, perhaps used for holding food caches or packs. It

The edge of the barren lands, near Smith Bay of Nueltin Lake.

is almost certainly the spot that Farley Mowat shared with his Métis trapper host while gathering material for *People of the Deer*. The gently sloping land on either side of the last stretch of the Windy River recalled for me his vivid sketch of the slaughter of caribou as they crossed the river.

Three old habitations in one day, if not an onslaught of humanity, suggested former sojourning and trading, a reasonable amount of life, a wayside for people travelling through. Now, except for a lone winter trapper or an occasional canoe party every five years or so, it is deserted.

We continued down Smith Bay and, as so often, saw Canada geese and goslings, but this time also two pairs of swans. The graceful birds were a stylish addition to a life filled with labour and enjoyment of the outdoors, but a life now routine, despite being divorced from our regular existence. The gentle hills – modest ones, for the most part rising about 200 feet above the water level – had for the last couple of days reminded me of tonsured heads, with a bald top surrounded by a fringe of small trees around the bottom. If the north slope is exposed to winds, then that part of the fringe is gone too. The land is by no means lush, but the green ground cover dominates the rocks and almost glows under the long evening sun. On a clear day in summer, the bare, gently undulating land and shining waters present an abiding serenity, an aspect of implacable calm.

We camped on an island, roughly kidney-shaped and a mile and a half long, on the north side of Smith Bay, close to its opening into Nueltin Lake. Gerd had caught a five-pound trout while trolling, and George used it to enhance our dinner. The site was quite rocky, but I found a reasonably level spot for our tent in a mossy area – soft, spongy moss it was, because it was basically a bog. One could step into water by forcefully stepping into an indentation in the moss. But Gerd liked the soft bed – he said that he could mould the moss to his body.

∗　　∗　　∗

The next day, overcast and with a cool breeze, showed a face of the north that was not so benign. We shivered in our wet feet as we ate lunch, and then it started to rain – a light but cold and driving rain. We saw ice on the shallow centre of the northern half of Nueltin and more ice towards the west in the distance, where the wind had driven it. People at Bill Bennett's lodge had reported seeing lots of ice in the open, northern part of Nueltin ten days earlier, when they had flown over to check conditions. It was now July 17, and we had been on the water for three weeks. Most trips would be over by now, but we had at least two more weeks, probably three, to go.

We kept heading north. And the day did change. The rain stopped and the breeze diminished. Although the weather was cloudy, it was no longer heavily overcast so the light made contrasting patterns as it emerged from heavily or lightly clouded areas. The leaden immensity of the lake exposed a variety of colour and texture in the sky. Grey, dark blue, light blue or an opalescent combination played on a field of sumptuously round clouds to the west, while streamers extended to the horizon in the north. The temperature was just right for paddling. The air felt substantial, tart and invigorating, and I revelled in the richness of the sky. I dug in with zest as we crossed large open stretches.

Gerd had been suffering from chapped hands. Paddling exposed our hands to the sun almost all the time, and they were frequently wet too – or at least one of them, if we held the paddle far enough down the shaft so that we immersed or splashed it as we drew the paddle through the water. Gerd had brought along lotions and even dishwashing gloves because he had sensitive hands. If his hands got too chapped, it would be like a hiker becoming lame. Luckily his problem did not get too serious.

When we stopped that evening, the temperature had fallen enough so that the breeze had a bite to it. I asked Dave what the temperature was – still 55°F, and the water, 44°F, just right for paddling with my light cashmere sweater under the rain jacket. We had done 35 miles that day on flat water and in good conditions. In camp, everyone put on dry socks and shoes. We then enjoyed one of our better meals – canned ham – but I added butter to the vegetable soup, to the dried sliced potatoes with some kind of sauce, and to the "brown Susan" – apples, raisins and crumbs served with lemon custard sauce. Hard work and a good day make a good meal better.

George's journal entry for this day, I later found out, reads simply: "Overcast all day chilly with some rain. The water temperature of Nueltin Lake is 44°F and some snow is seen on the shore. Long, tedious, point-to-point paddles are the order of the day. We camp at the north end, the bugs are bad and it is hard to find enough wood for supper."

To leave Nueltin and reach Seal Hole Lake we took the southern channel, the right-hand one, because it looked more direct than the northern one, and the map gave us no reason to choose between the rapids in the two channels. We stopped at the head of a small island and scouted the rapids. The water was thundering on its south and east side, while the other side had less flow but was long and boulder filled. We decided to carry the canoes along the middle of the almond-shaped island. The footing was firm, but that is all that one could say in its favour. A jumble of jagged rocks, some of them camouflaged by low scrub willows, invited a twisted ankle. To make matters worse, as I started to carry the kitchen pack – I like to take the heavier pack on the first trip – I discovered that I had not readjusted the shoulder straps from the longer lengths that George had used on a short lift earlier. So the pack rested low on my rump and pulled me back. Since I also carried our tent on top of the pack and the lunch pack of fifteen pounds was hanging from my neck in front of my chest, it did not seem worthwhile to unload everything to adjust the straps and then struggle to get upright again with that load. So I humped it all with the load hanging low on my butt. Blackflies like fast water, and they were legion. They liked me as I grunted and sweated and tottered for some 200 yards before I could drop the load at water's edge. I am sure that I inhaled some flies while gasping my way across. No portage is fun, but this was the worst short carry that I made. On the return trip and the next carry I used a head net. And thereafter I always made sure that pack straps suited me before I got upright under a load.

Another rapids faced us before Seal Hole Lake, and we ran these. Our splash cover, though snapped into place in the centre of the canoe, between front and rear thwarts, had not been battened down at the bow and stern because we wanted to give the paddlers legroom. In the process of ferrying over from the left side of the channel, which had some very heavy water, we ran through some turbulent current and shipped quite a bit of water. We went to shore and emptied the water before continuing on Seal Hole Lake, having descended 28 feet from Nueltin Lake.

At Seal Hole we had to battle a stiff north wind and a heavy chop. Each wave slapped high on our bow and splashed me. The exertions of the portage, having given way to the rush of running the rapids, now turned to the grind of putting our backs into each stroke. We did what we had to do and kept at it. The shore, low and covered with willows and dwarf spruce, was not inviting anyway. We did pick up some wood and carried it on top of the splash covers, since we planned to bake that night and our campsite might be barren. As we left Seal Hole Lake another task faced us: we climbed out of the canoes, waded through the shallow rapids and hauled the canoes by the gunwales or by a line. This work, never easy, became harder when my foot slipped off the basketball-sized boulders on the bottom of the stream.

We ate lunch at the top of a hill to enjoy the view – and to let the wind keep bugs at bay. It did that but also chilled us. Right at our lunch spot someone had built a windbreak for one, perhaps two people, by piling rocks or turning them on edge. The indentations were still in the soil from which the rocks had been lifted, but traces last a long time in the tundra. I imagined this as perhaps a blind from which Chipewyan hunters tracked caribou herds. Or maybe a canoeing party saw the place as a natural stop-

Whether called riffle or rapids, there are plenty of them in the north.

ping spot, as we did. We had no knowledge of any canoeists in this area in recent years, but there could have been the occasional one.

Evening camp, at the foot of a westward-facing quartz hill, gave a semblance of warmth in the setting sun. The air temperature was 50° F at 9:00 p.m. The camp, five yards above a narrow band of boulders that marked the water's edge, was on relatively flat ground on moss amid willows, so we did not need the wood that we had carried. The campfire was in a jumble of large rocks because George had found a rock with a large, flat, vertical face, which served as the back of the fireplace. It would reflect heat onto our pots and into the reflector oven. The canoes were upside down just inland of the band of rocks. The camp was blessedly free of bugs, either because of the wind or because it was colder and drier here. We draped various garments over the willows to dry. I took off my underpants, still wet from hauling the canoes up the shallow rapids, gave them a cursory wash and used them to decorate the top of a three-foot spruce, also festooned with my wet socks and sneakers. In that wind, my wool trousers dried quickly on my legs.

After taking care of clothing and camp chores, eating dinner, and an extra, post-prandial cup of tea for me, each of us went off at various times and in various directions to photograph or hike. Each person went alone – perhaps an understandable part of our dynamic. The fact that no one else was within, at best, a week's travel of us did not push us closer together. In the midst of an isolated wilderness, we spent plenty of time with each other in rather close quarters, while canoeing or in camp, and so we each enjoyed a solitary stroll. Certainly, it never entered my mind to seek company on this kind of occasion.

The light of the setting sun, almost amber, softened the landscape from the harsher one at lunch. From the hillside I saw splotches of water in all directions facing me, but now they gleamed and stood out from the gently contoured, almost featureless land that was gradually turning from a lush green to darkness. In that light and from a distance the ever-present rocks were not visible unless there was a prominent outcropping, like the one on which I stood.

After paddling a couple of miles the next morning and hauling the canoes up a short stretch of rocky rapids, we reached a small, nameless lake, about one mile wide and two miles long. A strong north wind was blowing in our faces and whipping spray from the tops of waves two feet high. George thought the wind too strong to battle, and everyone readily agreed. We put in on the right side and sought shelter behind a small grove of spruce trees, three or four feet tall, but compactly spaced. Standing up exposed us to the chilling wind, but a small clearing in the lee and plenty of wood made a cozy place to go literally to ground. We made a fire and everyone stripped off wet shoes and socks and placed them near the fire or hung them up in the little spruce to dry out in the wind. The gnarled root base of these small trees burned long, vigorously and aromatically. We heated the tea kettle and had an early lunch. Since we had not worked much that morning, everyone had only two slices of bread instead of the usual three, but no one skimped on the spreads, piling the slices high with peanut butter, honey, jam and butter – usually with three of the four. We also had a bit of cheese and some raisin and nut mixture. Afterwards people napped or dozed, lying on the moss with life vests as pillows and bare feet towards the fire.

The sky was grey and the wind felt cruel, especially given our wet feet and trousers, but life was pleasant enough in our little windbreak. We had a cozy fire, tea and plenty of food, so we took what the day allowed. Everyone had a chance to get extra sleep and to rest and catch up with journal entries. When I took a walk along the shore, the whipping wind and tender, bare feet soon drove me back into our clearing. It really was a day for holing up.

We stayed for about eight hours and then, around 6:30 p.m., became restless and moved out, even though the wind had not yet died down, but we hoped that it soon would. We headed north, into the wind, towards the Kognak River. The first couple of hours we consumed hauling the canoes up through a series of shallow rapids – we had to go into the water and wade while pulling the canoe with a line or by the gunwales. So our feet were immediately wet again. I never adjusted completely to having wet feet almost constantly. I tried to dry sneakers and socks, even though I knew that they would be wet again in a couple of hours. I made ungraceful leaps

Dave, Gerd and Peter taking advantage of the wind.

into or out of the canoe or tried to step on rocks on landing or launching just to save dry feet those relatively few times they were dry. The luxury of dry socks was reserved for camp in the evening. The wading and hauling that day were interspersed with brief stretches of paddling, but against a strong wind. Since we were working hard, the chilly evening did not bother us. The wind did diminish, and we entered some flat water and covered some miles in the gathering dusk.

Once again a stretch of hard work was redeemed. The only way to deal with a wind, a strong current or arduous portage was to plug away one step or stroke at a time. No matter how slowly a distant shore approached us as we dug paddles into the water, with a stiff wind blowing in our faces, or how ceaselessly one agonizing step followed another as we staggered across a portage, the end did get closer, one step at a time, and eventually arrive. As someone brought up with the riches of middle-class life and who never really had to struggle (school always came easily, for example), these were lessons that I have since retained, but I did wonder that perhaps forty might be rather a ripe age to be learning these things. Catastrophic hardship had hit my parents, uprooted from professional lives in their early thirties who fled their homeland of Latvia to make new lives with very young children in a new culture. But at the most stressful of those times I was an oblivious four, five, or six years old. I recognized what my parents had gone through; they still worked hard, but I had never had to – until now.

Of course, since we had no choice, since there was no alternative to reaching the other side of the lake or portage, we submitted with stoicism that one might not expect in other circumstances. The next question, then, is: why put oneself in these circumstances? Why would anyone voluntarily submit to such hardships and exhausting labour, "on vacation" yet? The reason lies in the rewards, many and multifarious. I hope that this account conveys my appreciation of those rewards. Many people who canoe in the north return again and again; they leave for the south each time with a melancholy sense of loss and eager to return.

One step at a time eventually forces you across the portage or up the rapids, just as one hard stroke at a time, bending forward and feeling the paddle flex as you dig into the water, brings up the next point of land. The distant shore gradually comes closer, and its details emerge. It seems tantalizingly near; you think that only 25 more strokes will take you to shore and to relieve you from paddling, and you count them out to yourself. But too often you find that you have been thinking wishfully, that it takes 75 strokes to reach land instead. And so, each hour and each day we inched forward. I imagined a map of our journey and drew satisfaction from our progress as we crawled across its face. By the end of this day we had travelled approximately 500 miles.

The end of the day came late, past 11:00 p.m., and after sunset. Once we stopped paddling, with my wet legs in the breeze and at a temperature of less than 50 degrees, I started shivering uncontrollably. I was as cold as I ever became on that trip. I had never before shivered like that. Thoughts of hypothermia and physical breakdown occurred to me as I hurriedly put on dry socks and sneakers and broke out, for the first time, a wool turtleneck held in reserve. With four layers on my torso – undershirt, turtleneck, light cashmere sweater and Gore-Tex anorak – I was warm in dry socks, even if not toasty, because the legs of my trousers were still wet.

The others had built a fire. Happily we had picked up wood earlier, so that we could choose a campsite regardless of its firewood supply – our spot was a flat, barren peninsula. I made dinner in the darkness. Everyone devoured it – a tribute less to the menu or to my cooking skill than to the caloric demands of the day. The situation had been uncomfortable, nasty even, but we had the equipment and the experience to come to terms with it, almost to make it comfortable. We retired to our rest, after 1:00 a.m., at that rocky northern shore and slept soundly.

CHAPTER 11

Kognak and Caribou

A BRIGHT AND CLOUDLESS MORNING promised a better day. We had our routines down pat and never lounged around in the morning so, as usual, were off into the canoes in good order. We paddled a few miles, made a short portage to a pond and paddled its three-quarter-mile length. We then looked over a longer portage to see if we could pick out a route that would most easily get us to the Kognak River. The portages in the barren lands are relatively easy. There are no trees and little brush – just pick a path to avoid as much muskeg and bog as possible. We skirted a couple of small ponds on the carry, deciding that the effort saved by paddling was not worth the trouble of loading and unloading, then we skirted low ground in which some small spruce were growing.

As we started the portage we saw our first caribou – a big one with a large rack. We were ready to admire it at length but it trotted over the hill. Further along we scared it up again. He pranced past the ponds in the crisp sunlight, carrying his antlers high, and continued over another rise to the northeast. We wondered why he was here when the major herds were considerably further north.

The portage of a little more than three-quarters of a mile took us to the Kognak River just above some rapids. The rapids were heavy but looked easy to run, and we started out. The water crashed and sparkled in the bright, crisp air. As we rounded a corner, a pair of ducks scrambled out from under us and flew off. The roar of the rapids had masked our approach. A delightful two-mile run eastward emptied us into Hawk Hill Lake.

On the lake we headed northeast into a brisk north wind. We had to work for more than six miles into that wind, with the quartering waves slapping the canoe and splashing me frequently. I tried – with moderate success – to time my stroke so that I could dig into an oncoming wave and pull the canoe towards it before it could curl over the bow. I chopped down on each wave, as if it were my enemy, and pulled the canoe to the crest. Eventually a peninsula on the north side of the lake did provide a lee, a welcome respite and a place for lunch. Then we turned north.

The northeast arm of the lake ends in wild rapids more than a mile long, but straight, free of rocks and not hard to run. Our splash covers had been buttoned down for the lake crossing, and we charged into the rapids after examining them briefly from the shore. An exhilarating roller-coaster ride ended too quickly as the river broadened into Mountain Lake.

We made an early camp at 4:30 p.m. at the foot of the unnamed mountain that gives the lake its name. The mountain rises some 650 feet above the lake and had been prominent all day. Since the weather was still beautiful and we had lots of time, everyone busied himself with housekeeping chores or equipment repair. George sewed up the crotch of his pants, which he had ripped the previous day while making a large stride as we hauled the canoe up rapids. David's canvas shoes had suffered tears on portages and rapids, so he set to sewing them up. Gerd cut his hair and beard with a tiny pair of scissors, and I retaped a seam in the armpit of my Gore-Tex jacket with seam sealer. The leak had let water in as I lifted my arm during our run through the high waves in the rapids. Some water may have entered also during the paddle against the wind on Hawk Hill Lake.

The original seam had come loose under my right arm – that side rather than the left probably because we paddled more on my left side, a stroke during which one lifts the right arm high and stretches it forward. I estimated that we covered seven feet with each stroke, so that travelling more than 500 miles to date had required some 440,000 strokes. The right arm might well have gone through its high motion some 300,000 times and, of course, we did more than just paddling. And there was more to come.

After chores, there was still time for other tasks or recreation. The pleasant weather and abundant firewood encouraged bread baking – usually a time-consuming task. Moreover, the fireplace had a large flat vertical rock behind it, which efficiently directed heat into the reflector oven, so we baked two batches of bread – four loaves. Dave mixed and baked one batch, and George made the other.

After dinner, Gerd and I hiked up the mountain, separately and at different times. Dave too went on a saunter after baking. The hill – or mountain, by local standards – is round and bald. Of course everything around these parts is bald – rocky or with low ground cover. Small spruce occur rarely, in sheltered, south-facing declivities. The view from the hill was welcome and uplifting after the two-dimensional perspective of our canoes. Everywhere I looked I saw splotches of water interspersed with blotches of land, one the negative of the other. It looked like an infinite variety of ink blots arrayed in all directions. One could impose some order on the landscape by an effort of will, by looking for major lakes or watercourses, although the path of rivers was not always discernible. One way to transcend the bewildering reality, to contain it, was to connect our voyage to maps, to plans drawn by human beings on paper. The tangle of rivers and lakes then collapsed to a few square inches on the map, which we could hunch over and, thus, dominate at least the symbol of the wilderness. From the maps we could also assure ourselves that they do eventually extend to areas that contain towns and roads.

Another way to deal with the intractable was to push it farther away. By considering it the land "just beyond the fence," we rendered it something of which we were somewhat aware, but that we did not need to know since it was not of us. One can ignore the wild – divorce oneself from it – whether one is in the city or in the midst of the wilderness. Of course, the latter requires a more drastic, almost schizophrenic, disconnection. Or one can let the otherness of the wilderness be so alienating as to unhinge one. Each stance – denying it, ignoring it or allowing it to confound – arises when the individual is disconnected from wild nature. That person may enjoy the outdoors in some manner, but I wonder how deeply he or she can, for example, savour the tundra under the soft evening light, watching as the earth tones glow, then darken, as watery surfaces first glisten and then become islands of light in a surrounding darkness. That person may also strike out and curse at the blackflies and mosquitoes that have come to join him or her on a still evening.

I had taken my journal along on the half-mile climb, intending to spend a reflective evening writing and enjoying the view from on high. Sitting there, 600 feet above the camp, I started to write, but the wind died down, even on top of the hill, and the bugs came out. Well, we had had a respite from them for a couple of days. Although they were not as bad this evening as they had been earlier, I still returned to the tent to write. Another very good day – sunny, great rapids, no long labours, only ten miles covered (all downhill), good scenery, a relaxing evening.

We had been seeing a couple of DC-3 airplanes each day for a few days and would continue to see them; they supplied a gold mine at Cullaton Lake, five miles north of the bend in the Kognak River. I greeted the sight and sound of them according to my mood. If I was weary and disheartened, they were a reminder of a civilized world out there somewhere, and also that the mine could be a resource if we were in trouble. More often, I resented them as intrusions into our pristine wilderness. Even more disturbing, we had seen claim stakes, topped by brightly coloured plastic ribbons, two days in a row. But for the most part we were alone; we heard only the sound of water lapping against the canoe or rushing down a rapid, as well as the wind in its expressive variety and, frequently, birds.

* * *

Each person heard his own hard breathing in the morning as we crossed the five or six miles of Mountain Lake northeastward against a breeze. Then we re-entered the Kognak River. The contour lines on the map indicated a strong and rapid flow. The river was not only steep but also went on and on. A drop of four feet per mile creates what are considered gentle rapids, whereas the Kognak falls 170 feet in the ten miles between Mountain Lake and Ducker Lake. This stretch of the Kognak had the most dangerous rapids on the trip and, before we set out on the river, George gave us a cautionary talk and instructions.

We buttoned down the splash cover on the canoe, wetting it so that we could stretch it over the gunwales. (The nylon when stretched and buttoned down dries drum tight.) I tightened and snapped everything on my Gore-Tex coat and put on my lifejacket snugly. I put clip-ons made of Polaroid material onto my glasses to see water hazards better in the glare. I climbed into the bow cockpit, gathered up the loose nylon skirt and belted it around my chest with the bungee-cord drawstring. I made sure that it was good and tight, since on earlier occasions water had entered the top of the skirt and had slid down my rain jacket to settle in my lap.

The idea was to create a kayak-like craft, with everything sealed off from the water and our two upper torsos sealed within, but sitting above, the integral nylon. It usually works well, but some water commonly does get inside at the drawstring. Most of it stays out and flows down the skirt. The drawstring starts out at chest height but, as bigger waves hit, the water settles on top of the loose skirt around the waist and pulls the skirt downward. I then pull on the top of the skirt to flip the water – sometimes two or three gallons – out of my lap and out of the canoe. In this case the scale of the river and George's cautionary comments caused me to prepare carefully – and a bit apprehensively too.

Once we started down the river, apprehensions and any time to spare for them disappeared. We hurtled down; some stretches were a gallop down a steep sluice – simple, but so fast compared to our usual pace that I was both delighted at our easy progress and troubled that this terrific river was passing too fast. Other stretches were as rough and as violent as any on the trip so far; the waves bounced and buffeted us as if playing with us, then suddenly attacked to smite us or to throw us out of the river. We sought out the calmer channels, trying to avoid large standing waves and haystacks, but there was no avoiding all the violent water. We picked out smooth "Vs" to descend, but they soon turned into standing waves two, four, even five feet high, occasionally seven feet from crest to trough. The canoe climbed some waves and bucked merrily along, but others were penetrated with the bow. And since I was two or three feet behind the bow, such waves smashed me in the chest, sometimes so hard that it took my breath away. At a sharp bend in the river the current bounced off the rocky walls and the crossing currents set up waves like sharp moguls on a ski slope. They came from every direction. In one place where the river made a turn of more than 90 degrees, the water was even more confused and treacherous and, as a consequence, frightening. We chose the quieter inside of the bend and bounced through with the decks no more awash than at other places on the Kognak.

In relatively level stretches between bodies of whitewater, we pulled to shore into an eddy, holding onto rocks, to wait for the other canoe. These quieter moments allowed me to reflect on the river, which slid by us in the crisp sunlight while its roar from above and below remained ever-present. Then the ride continued; back in the saddle, we hurtled into the tumult. We again hit wild water. The waves thumped me while the canoe slid sideways and I lost my balance, flinging my arms akimbo. I thought that I would lose my paddle, holding it in one hand above my head, but I recovered and we thundered on. Losing the paddle could have serious consequences. Since I helped provide motive power and steering, George might not be able to control the canoe by himself. We could have dumped, losing gear and food, and possibly developed hypothermia – or even drowned.

The water tossed, pushed and pulled us. Water is heavy and gravity is inexorable. The two combined into an awesome display, whose primeval power one can feel only from within the midst of the torrent. What might look like a frothy current from a distance, or even from a nearby shore, becomes an implacable force when one is tossing about in it. We could deflect our direction somewhat, and we could speed up or slow down relative to the current, but for the most part we simply had to go with it. The saving factor was another force of nature: our buoyancy. It is hard to drown a cork. In open canoes, without our splash covers, the ride would have been utterly impossible.

We slid down, we were bounced around, and a couple of times we rested. But most of the time we lived completely in the moment; the ride passed in a blur of adrenaline. And a spectacular, exhilarating ride it was – a clear river with no boulders, thickets of rocks or shallow water. The entire length was runnable. The previous day had been very fine for running rapids, but this one was incomparable, even for George, who had had plenty of experience. (If the Kognak River were within 500 miles of a population centre, rather than in Nunavut, it would be a renowned whitewater river.) Too suddenly, it was over, and we were in Ducker Lake. How long did it take? Maybe an hour, including stops.

When we reached the lake we had a pleasant surprise. The wind, which had been our opponent, now decided to help us as we headed south-eastward, and at such a brisk rate that it was worthwhile to put up a sail. We had two rain flies that we used as cooking and camp shelters. We put one of them up as a sail between the canoes, which now formed a loose catamaran. Gerd and I – the two bowmen – tied a corner of the fly to the butt end of our paddles and wrapped the short length of the fly around the shaft of each paddle. We then placed the blade on the bottom of the canoe in front of us, propping it with our feet. We stretched the rain fly between the canoes, each of us holding our bottom corner of the sail against the paddle or tying it down. A line tied from the top or butt end of the paddle ran towards the stern seat of each canoe to brace the paddles against the wind. The sternmen kept the two canoes pointing slightly outward from each other. Each of the four men loosened or tightened the sail according to wind gusts. And we sailed merrily along.

I lounged in my seat, held my corner of the sail and revelled in our rapid progress, and even more in its ease. For a venture that often yielded progress only grudgingly and after great effort, this was a blessed largesse that lasted ten or twelve miles. Our previous stretch of sailing, on Wollaston Lake, had covered only two or three. While we scudded along, George and Gerd trolled for fish and soon caught three lake trout. The then wind changed direction, so we took down the sail and resumed paddling.

Dave and Gerd pulled a mile and a half ahead of us, and after a while George realized that they should have turned left and gone slightly north of east to continue on Ducker Lake, whereas they had held to a south-easterly direction and were about to enter another lake. A 25-degree turn to the left should have corrected our course. The error is straightforward to describe, but from the canoes these bodies of water did not look distinct, and no significant landmarks such as tall hills guided us. Consequently, a lapse in attention easily led to a missed turn. We made the turn back, having gone a mile out of the way, and pretty soon caught the attention of the others, who also turned. A global positioning system (GPS) would have been helpful, but it was not yet in place.

It was now 7:00 p.m. and I raised an issue that had been bothering me. As we had had a great day – paddling against the wind on Mountain Lake, a splendid run down the Kognak, the bounty of the sailing on Ducker Lake, with 26 miles traversed – I thought that we should stop for the night. After outlining these factors to George, I ended by saying, "I think we spend too many days scrambling from dawn to dusk. Let's stop and reflect on this great day, and just enjoy the north."

"We should continue and get to the end of Ducker Lake," George replied. "Then we'll be off the lake and back sheltered in the Kognak River. You know I think we should make time while we can. If a wind comes up we could sit for as long as a week."

We had spoken of this before. On other trips George had been windbound for long spells. I agreed with the theory but thought that we practised it too stringently. On this occasion I was also well aware that it was my turn to cook, and I did not relish the prospect of preparing food in the dark again, particularly since I had to clean the fish first. The other two agreed with George, and we pushed on. I respect George's experience and competence enormously, but I think that he himself could enjoy the north even more than he does. I again wondered about Gerd and Dave's enthusiasm for the whole project and suspected that they would just as soon not prolong it.

We made camp at 10:00 p.m., having covered, with the aid of the Kognak and the favourable wind, a record 36 miles. We had surpassed 30 miles on other days, but only by putting in a lot of time on flat water. The camp tonight was on an isolated point at the north end of Ducker Lake. The threatening weather made George fearful of the high winds that can occur in these parts, so he and Gerd pegged the tents extra tight and weighted down the corners of the rain flies with large boulders. George also helped me clean the fish. The smallest one got washed away and lost in the twilight. I then fried them in place of our planned main course of millet goulash. There was plenty to eat. I made dessert in the dark. But we almost lost that too because Dave, eager to do the dishes – no easy task in the dark – so that he could go to bed almost washed out the dessert pot before we had eaten it.

After midnight all the kitchen tasks were done, and everyone rushed off to bed as a slight drizzle started. But I lit up my cigar and said to myself that now I was going to enjoy the time. I sat down with a cup of tea and leaned against an upturned canoe, and I decided that it was a fine evening. I was snug in my jacket and hat against the light rain. The Kognak rustled and chuckled in front of me as it flowed out of Ducker Lake and resumed its irregular course eastward and northward – a course that we had been delighted to follow. We looked forward to more of it. I thought about the day and about living in the north, and a feeling of well-being came over me. I felt good about the day and about being comfortable, even sitting in the rain.

*   *   *

The next morning was again crisp and clear – "another day in paradise," as the TV weathermen in Florida like to say in the winter. But the Subarctic competes with Florida winters in hours of sunshine. The temperatures do not compare, but there is very little rain in the far north The Kognak was now wider and milder, but with a strong current. We ran some rapids and carried our canoes around a ledge. George told me that he agreed about our scrambling hurry – for example, he was a week behind in his diary. He said that this day should be short, and perhaps also the next one. Later I noticed on his map that he had marked "nice camp?" at some rapids about fifteen miles downriver, so he had been thinking of the site some time earlier. We did stop there.

When we started paddling George told me to take it easy, and we soon fell behind Dave and Gerd. They pulled further and further ahead, until they stopped to wait for us. When we caught up, Dave was agitated and said, "I am not prepared to dilly-dally. There are a number of things about the trip I'm not satisfied with, and I don't want to prolong the trip."

He continued in one outburst to say that he was prepared to fly out at his (considerable) expense by going to the mine or trying to find the prospecting helicopter that we had spotted. George started to get heated too but restrained himself, partly because I urged him not to let things escalate. He took a dig at Dave's navigation error that had cost us a mile or two the previous day. Everybody realized that if Dave were to quit it would destroy the remainder of the trip; it would cause such difficulty that I, for one, could not put much credence in his threat. No one wanted to continue the wrangling, and the canoes soon separated. When we stopped for lunch, there were desultory attempts at idle conversation. Dave, unusually, ate very little. At 4:00 p.m. we camped early at the rapids that George had marked on his map.

I had been surprised by the intensity of Dave's outburst, but not by his dissatisfaction. Dave was the most convivial of the four of us; we other three, satisfied to live within ourselves, were taciturn to a fault. I sometimes felt that Dave was put off by the lack of meaningful exchanges and of any growing friendships. Gerd and I had minimal conversation in the tent at night. We were usually too tired to do anything other than sleep and, I suspect, Dave and George were the same. Some conversation did take place in camps between the four of us, usually about the events and setting of our travels, but we had lots of chores, so we had no long, engaging talks around the fire. The best time for extended discussions was during long paddles on flat water, but the two canoes were rarely within conversing distance of each other. George and I had some, but we shared adolescence and physics. We did converse in the canoe – about the trip itself, about George's experiences in the north, about physics research and faculty politics – but long periods of silence were fine for me, and for George. In fact, once when discussing canoeing, George told me that he did not like to have a partner who chattered, which I took as an impersonal, neutral and perfectly understandable comment. Whatever else might have upset Dave, I felt that the voyage was not measuring up to what he wanted in terms of socializing or friendship.

I knew that the four of us would not change, nor would the character of the trip, but I made an effort to speak to Dave and to let him know that he was not alone. I agreed with him that the tempo of that day should not be the norm, but I added that we should enjoy what we had, that it had taken a lot of effort to reach where we were, and that we should not rush out. I did have a qualm or, at most, two that I might have been the cause of the disruption, that George might have slowed down at my request. The others too spoke to Dave. There was a conciliatory mood in camp, and Dave did not renew any suggestions about flying out, which would have been very difficult and expensive. George said that he had planned for six weeks, with an additional week possible for emergencies, and he did not want to finish in five weeks just because we had been making good time. He did say that five and a half weeks would be fine with him.

Since the day was sunny and a fine breeze kept most of the bugs at bay, everyone bathed, but expeditiously, since the water was cold and the breeze brisk. My last bath about a week earlier had been in colder water and with more bugs present, so I washed my hair a little more thoroughly – and also my underwear, my T-shirt and the bandana that I wore around my neck. Everything dried in short order while I wore my pyjama tops as a shirt. I wanted to keep clean and to dry my one spare shirt. The newly laundered clothing smelled antiseptic in contrast to its musty, damp and mouldy odour of the previous few days when I had used shaving cream as detergent. My tube of shaving cream had been punctured, so I used a portion of it for the laundry – after all, we reserved shaving for only the warmest and most leisurely occasions.

As I was putting up the tent and trying to decide how to orient it, I realized that the opening should face the wind to discourage bugs from

Dave and Gerd walking their canoe up the Tha-Anne.

accompanying us in. I should have thought of that earlier, although local topography mostly determines placement of the tent. The guiding factor is finding as smooth a sleeping surface as possible.

George, who had been cooking, cheerily called out, "Dinner is ready, a multi-course extravaganza! Lentil soup is now being served!"

We dug in and enjoyed the soup and the main course – a concoction of rice, wild rice, vegetables and some kind of meat. Dessert was fruit and tapioca pudding and, as usual, everything was made from dehydrated stuff. As an extra, George had made a pancake in the reflector oven. The camp was cozy; a canoe had been brought up and turned on its side to act as windbreaker for the fireplace, and for anyone interested in a sheltered place to sit. I located a comfortable seat some distance away on the rocks, arranging for myself a backrest and a seat upholstered with the Ensolite sleeping pad. I had another large rock for an armrest and I sat in that armchair near the rushing rapids and enjoyed the evening sun. The sun spotlighted our tents – an orange one and a green one, the most vivid objects in the land-

Sometimes you don't paddle or portage – you just have to drag the canoe upstream.

scape. The tents were at the foot of a slight rise, where small spruce had found shelter. The small rise and our descent of about 250 feet since Seal Hole Lake provided enough protection for the scrub trees to eke out an existence. When Dave dug out his thermometer and announced that the temperature was 54°F, I was surprised that I was so comfortable in that temperature and in the wind. Of course, we sported our anoraks against the wind most of the time, but I wore only one layer under it. We really were acclimated. Dave pronounced the water to be 50 degrees, which was cool, but not as cool as it had felt during the brief bath a little earlier.

✳   ✳   ✳

We continued next morning down the Kognak, flowing fast and smoothly in a direction slightly south of east. We saw fluffy yellow goslings, about the size of small chickens, scampering along the shore. No parents were in sight; perhaps the chicks had reached the age of independence, but they were still flightless. Many times we had seen adult ducks and Canada geese trying to distract us from their offspring. Sometimes the goose would think that it was leading us a merry chase, quacking and flapping its wings, as it preceded us in the direction in which we wanted to go. The river here was a channel between high walls. We stopped and climbed a thirty-foot bank to take a look at the countryside, but we could not see much but low ground stretching into greyness. When we descended, some goslings in confusion began to run uphill towards us through the willows on the shore. We could not resist catching a couple. They indeed were fuzzy and served as nice hand warmers for a minute or so before we released them.

Lunch was to be at the confluence of the Kognak with the Tha-Anne River. From a distance, we saw what looked like tents and some red object, partly obscured behind a rise. It turned out to be an airplane. We found four fishermen and their pilot, all fishing for trout and grayling in the fast water. One of the fishermen was from Texas, while all the others were from Saskatoon. They had flown in two days earlier and said that half an hour after they landed a party of three canoes had gone down the Kognak. The canoe party had flown in and had been going for 300 miles. They were to be picked up by plane a day or two later. Their route certainly included some nice downhill runs. We had lunch some distance from the fisher-men, but they were easily in view in this open country, which was not as isolated as some of us had hoped. Aircraft have certainly opened up the north; mines, prospectors, fishermen, hunters and eco-tourists all depend crucially on planes or helicopters. Occasionally they leave no sign of their passage, but some evidence is inevitable – most frequently oil barrels, either in caches or empty and discarded and drifting ashore on some otherwise-pristine lake. Empty 55-gallon drums are known as the litter of the north.

After lunch I found a comfortable spot in the lee of some large boul-ders and, facing what sun there was, napped for an hour. George went off on an unsuccessful search for signs of old Indian or Inuit campsites. When I awoke, I saw Gerd fishing and, because of plenty of signs of fish surfac-ing, I joined in. Not a nibble for my offerings, but Gerd soon caught a five-pound trout and then a fifteen-pounder. The latter was a fat pig of a trout and more than sufficed for an excellent chowder that George made that evening.

After the stop, we made a sharp turn northward and went up the Tha-

Anne River. It is a broad, open stream, but in some parts the current was too fast for paddling, so we walked the canoes up or lined them. The going was much easier than during previous upstream hauls because now we had no rocks or shallows to wrestle the canoes around or over; we could walk in the stream or on the low, level bank, impeded only by the clear current. We hiked for a mile and a half, pulling the canoes along the edge of the broad stream, and our feet got a good cleaning.

CHAPTER 12

South Henik Lake

THE CLOUDS DISSIPATED AND THE emerging sun gave a pleasant brown and dun cast to our flat, treeless surroundings. We resumed paddling, reached Roseblade Lake, swung around its eastern side for five miles, and entered a channel on its northeast corner that would lead to South Henik Lake. A sheltered cove below an esker on the west side of the channel attracted us as a likely campsite. Upon landing we found that it had attracted other travellers over the years. We saw a number of Inuit tent rings – rocks placed in a circle ten feet in diameter, where they had held down tents. Lichens on the rocks and lichens continuing undisturbed on the gravel indicated tent sites many decades old. On top of the esker we also found a small pile of rocks built up into a cairn. A tin can there contained a note from G. Slater and a companion who, in 1969, had made the same journey from Reindeer Lake to Eskimo Point that we were doing. A more recent but anonymous visitor had added, "Good Luck. 1977." George left a note with our names.

These signs of other travellers struck a chord and connected us to our fellows, who had arrived by water or dogsled. I did not feel the same link to the fly-in fishermen whom we had met earlier, living beings though they were, and happy as we had been to greet them.

I tried to write my log every day to record impressions fresh, and, except when we had had a long and busy day, I succeeded. That evening, while writing in the tent, I not only felt a chill, but saw my breath condense. I called out to Dave for a reading – 42 degrees!

* * *

When we rose at 6:20 the temperature was 48°F and the sky was overcast, but the air was still. We were embarking northward to travel the length of South Henik Lake, 60 miles of water that is an open expanse for its upper two-thirds, where it widens out to fifteen miles. We had had great luck with large lakes so far and we hoped that the overcast skies, and the slight drizzle that soon started, would keep the wind down. They did and we made good progress. When we reached the narrows just before the lake opens up, a surprising current met us. The narrowest place was a mile wide and, with a depth of two feet, very shallow. One could expect to fight winds on lakes, but I resented the unexpected current after we had fought it for 45 minutes. A couple of low peninsulas projected from the west side of the narrows and, on their north sides, we saw a tumble of stove-sized boulders piled twenty feet high. We figured that we were seeing an example of the power of the prevailing north winds which, when combined with the current, could bulldoze ice floes into and up the shallows during break-up.

We made a lunch stop at one of these points, and a chilly meal it was – as usual, we were wet, the wind was blowing and it was cool and overcast. No firewood of any kind was in sight; so, for one of the few times on the trip, we used the small backpackers' gas stove we had brought along for these kinds of situations. The hot broth was just what we needed. But we did not tarry; a big lake still awaited and paddling was the best way to stay warm.

After we finished, the overcast broke up, and we enjoyed two hours of fine paddling. But then the north wind picked up, and then blew up even more, while we were on the most open part of the lake, though close to the western shore. We still had twenty miles to travel in completely exposed water and into the teeth of that wind, so we went ashore at 4:30 to wait for calm. To the north and east of us lay open blue-green water decorated with series of white caps; only to the northwest were distant hills apparent. Looking to the west and south we could see almost as far across low ground, the tundra undulating with dull green swells.

We hauled the canoes and gear some 30 yards up the beach and made camp at the base of a sand bank, in the shelter of which subsisted some dwarf spruce and scrub willow. We used the canoes to shelter the campsite from the wind. We turned one over and placed the other next to it, but on its side and at 120 degrees to the first. This "V" embraced the fire about twelve feet away. We tied down the overturned canoe with a splash cover.

Dave and Peter making the wind-bound camp on South Henik Lake.

Some of our large packs, placed inside each canoe, also stabilized them. We had supper and hoped to paddle during an evening calm. But the wind continued strong and the breaking waves on our beach maintained their rhythm, so at 9:00 we put up the tents and waited for the next day.

The morning was just as windy and threatening clouds were out too. So we developed our site further by rigging a rain and wind shelter. We pulled a rain fly, staked down behind the canoe lying on its side, over towards the fireplace and supported it at its upper, open end with paddles so as to form an awning. A light rain did fall, but briefly, and the day soon cleared completely, although the wind kept up its force. Since we were well set up and had no place to go, and some wood was available, we decided to bake. George and Dave worked together – a departure from our kitchen pairing. Dave became very animated and discussed baking and other camp crafts at length with George.

We had had supper here the previous night and now, after breakfast, lunch, plenty of tea during the day, and baking four loaves of bread, we

114

were imposing serious firewood demands upon this barren spot. I even shaved, for the third time on the trip, because we had leisure and hot water. We used what dead wood there was but also sacrificed a number of scrub spruce. The most effective way to gather such small trees, less than two feet high, was to rip them from the sandy soil by pulling on the exposed roots. The gnarled base and root system together were four or five times the mass of the exposed tree, suggesting a hard life for plants at these latitudes – and very old survivors. We burned the entire trees, roots and all, but I wondered whether I was destroying something that had managed to grow for 50 years before we arrived.

We were used to eating large meals – "gross" would describe them better – and we had had three while doing nothing but lying about on the wind-bound beach. Feeling fat and sluggish, I went for a long walk along the shore. The bright windy afternoon in completely open country reminded me of days on the high plains of eastern Colorado or Wyoming, but here immense expanses of water spread all about me. The lake stretched without limit to both the northeast and to the south. To the north and northwest distant hills, the only elevations in sight, did tantalize the observer. If we could reach them we could paddle eastward in their lee regardless of the north wind. I walked in that empty openness for some three miles under an enormous sky. The campsite behind me was the only feature on the landscape. It remained distinct but decreased to a speck when I glanced back, walking between the blue flatness of the lake on my right and the almost flat tundra on my left. The ground, which looked dull green from a distance, on closer inspection sported a low ground cover that displayed a profusion of speck-like pink and purple flowers.

In that emptiness, I was surprised to find driftwood strewn along the shore, not from deadfalls that the wind and currents might have carried from a forested place, but milled pieces uniformly one inch square and three feet long, grey and weathered. I gathered up a large armful and carried it to camp, then went back to pick up most of the rest in another armful. We knew of a fly-in fishing lodge between North and South Henik Lakes that might have been the source of the wood. Its use was a mystery, as the wood had no nail marks. But its regular size would allow convenient bundling and carrying in our canoes. Like other industrial artifacts this wood seemed an intrusion, and I gathered it up as litter, but also as an unexpected bounty.

That civilization adds to life, by easing toil or discomfort, is one of its defining qualities. And here we were working hard to distance ourselves from it, or at least from mechanized urban life, to such an extent that I resented any example of it impinging upon our wilderness. Yet I happily grasped the conveniences that it provided. To compound the contradictions, how could I consider such objects intrusive when we were imposing our presence here, even ravaging the scant vegetation for our ease? Although I felt some guilt about ripping out the scrub trees, at heart I did not believe that I was violating the place. Rather, I had come to be more and more comfortable under any of the circumstances that we had encountered; I felt at home. I realized that I wanted to preserve the place but thought that I had a right to use it and to behave as I needed, much like other stewards, or husbanders, of resources.

I was there partly for respite from profligate consumption, but that is not to say that I wanted to escape completely from civilized life. Civilization expands possibilities, opening realms of expression and feeling. And that

The barren lands.

116

is what was happening to us. Our isolation and intimate contact with nature connected us to something essential, perhaps primordial – akin to an experience of art. In short, we are of nature and of culture – each speaks to us, provides for us, extends us.

At 5:00 p.m. the wind, though still brisk, diminished enough that bugs – mosquitoes only, not the annoying blackflies – made a tentative reappearance. We were all getting restless; we hoped to paddle that evening. George assumed that we would and took down his tent, and the others started to pack. The wind did die down, and we set out at 7:30. Everything was trimly packed and tucked under splash covers in preparation for the lengthy evening paddle across open water. A compact bundle of wood, lying on top of the covers, broke the sleek line of each canoe.

The days were rapidly getting shorter and sunset arrived soon after we were on the lake, suddenly glassy smooth. The sun, fat and orange, went down through a red and purple sky and settled into the hills in the northwest corner of the lake. That corner turned a deeper orange and then a red, while the opposite side of the lake, the east, became darker and darker. At one point, before everything dimmed out, the eastern sky and the lake were the same deep blue, separated by a thin line of dark grey that marked the low land on the east shore. We enjoyed the sunset and paddled by starlight into the stillness, the only sounds those of paddles dipping into the water and the swirl and chuckle of the eddy at the end of each stroke.

After an hour or so, other sounds came from around us – ripples and gurgles in the water. Trout were surfacing. The water would roil; a fin would appear and then submerge. Occasionally the same fish played on the surface two or three times before disappearing. The trout were all around us. Gerd could not resist the temptation. He assembled his rod, cast two or three times and caught a pair of five-pounders. Then we heard other sounds on the lake too. From the darkness ahead we heard a motorboat and voices, and we came on two motorboats from the lodge at the head of the lake. They were out with their guests for some midnight fishing. We chatted briefly and paddled on. Eventually we bumped into the shore and made a quick camp. I made a light supper of soup and dessert, and we were in bed at 1:00 a.m.

*   *   *

Dave, Gerd, Peter and George on a hilltop at the north end of South Henik Lake.

That evening we had aimed for the tallest hill on the north shore, intending to climb it the next day, and we tried to hold that course through the darkness, but in the morning we found that we had ended up two miles east of where we wanted to be. Over the course of some nineteen miles and five hours of paddling, three of them in darkness, we had strayed eastward. The peak, at 1,155 feet above sea level, was almost 600 feet above the lake. As the tallest thing for twenty miles in any direction, and conveniently situated next to the shore, it was a prominence that we just had to climb.

We broke camp in leisurely fashion and left at 10:00 a.m. to paddle back to the foot of the hill. A hike of two miles took us very gradually upward over expanses of flat grey rock. The area, almost empty of grasses and lichens, was a moonscape of slick hard rock. An arctic hare jumped out and leapt away. I thought that it should have been able to find a more hospitable environment. But it was not the only one to find the hill to its liking,

118

for at the top we came upon two sandhill cranes. They were walking along and croaking to each other but flew off when they noticed us, no doubt astonished at the appearance of human beings in the immense emptiness.

The ground beneath our feet was rocky and barren; one would think that we were in arid and desolate country. But when I lifted my view, quite a different aspect appeared. Half of what the eyes beheld was water. The hill is on a narrow isthmus between North and South Henik Lakes. On either side of us enormous sheets of water glistened in the bright sunlight. In the other directions the land, as usual, was splattered with a myriad of smaller lakes, irregular and random, extending as far as the eye could see. The landscape lay placid and serene. A gentle breeze caressed us, but nothing stirred, nothing was visible but water, rock and tundra. As in our previous climbs, the change of perspective from the surface along which we had been crawling to this elevated, three-dimensional view was expansive spiritually, as well as physically. This time the air seemed clearer and the sun brighter. We could see farther and in more detail. We could encompass and embrace more of our environment. It was a grand place for lunch. We remarked on the panorama, but only cursorily, because words could add little. I thought us more contemplative than usual, perhaps because the vastness emphasized our solitude.

CHAPTER 13

Tim Hortons and Ptarmigan

R ETURNING TO THE CANOES WAS like going back to a work-a-day world. We paddled east a few miles to the lodge at the channel between North and South Henik Lakes. And thus began an afternoon of intensive socializing in the Northwest Territories. The lodge was just a couple of simple buildings, sufficient to feed and accommodate guests who flew in to fish. A large airplane with the logo of Tim Hortons coffee shops sat disabled on the gravel airstrip, awaiting parts. A floatplane, used for ferrying fishing clients to nearby lakes, stood in readiness. A helicopter was moving oil drums at the far end of the strip. Ptarmigan, with their bright red rings around their eyes, walked as peacefully as hens around the camp and around the wheels of the airplane. George spoke to a party of fishermen who were about to take the floatplane on a trip to Dubawnt Lake, which George had canoed a few years earlier.

The managers of the lodge, Karl and Marsha Mohr, both in their early thirties, greeted us warmly and were eager to talk. Over coffee we found that they spend three or four months each summer at the fishing camp and then do a variety of things in the winter. For the upcoming winter, they planned to go bicycling in New Zealand. They offered us showers, which we declined for reasons not at all clear, since we were by no means clean. I worried that a warm shower would wrench me back to the soft life (and, again, I found the heated cabin stuffy); a considerable trip still lay ahead of us, and we would soon be just as dirty. No one else accepted the offer either. Our hosts asked if we needed anything else and we were happy to accept fresh oranges and four bottles of beer for the road.

We paddled four miles to the northeast corner of the lake and then portaged for a half-mile over a slight rise of land into Ameto Lake. Across the width of the lake we could see the mineral exploration camp to which the helicopter at the fishing camp had returned. We paddled the mile or so over to chat with them. They turned out to be young guys – students and recent geology graduates – spending the summer in the area using detailed helicopter surveys to explore for Esso Minerals. Some of them spent ten days or two weeks at a time away from the base camp, at "fly camps." They said that the Maguse River, for which we were heading, had at least one ferocious set of rapids.

The leader of the group was close-mouthed and suspicious of us, particularly when he found that we were scientists. He probably thought that people would come to these barren lands only on business – the same business as his. But eventually he and everyone warmed to the idea – strange as it may have seemed – that we were there for "fun." They plied us with coffee. They confirmed what we had learned at the fishing lodge – in June the area had been overrun by a caribou herd that now had moved further north. They did think that we would see some caribou. They also gave us four more bottles of beer. It was as if we were collecting a tax of beer from everyone who had flown into the territory.

Seeing all these people and airplanes was again both a pleasant change and a disturbance. I had become so accustomed to our solitude that the appearance of people and their possessions forced me to acknowledge the other world. Despite being unnerving, the social contact at the lodge and at the exploration camp relieved tensions perhaps building up owing to our isolation. (Though generally subdued, tensions had surfaced, as we saw above.) George and Dave's baking session at the wind-bound camp had brought the two of them together and raised congeniality in general. And so we had an unexpected day of socializing in the wilderness at 62°N – both jarring and a relief. But the change of pace soon passed, as the enormous tract of water, rock and tundra swallowed up reminders of our usual life.

A few miles eastward, out of sight and sound of the exploration camp and with a diminishing consciousness of it, we camped at a narrow part of Ameto Lake. Our visitors that night were a couple of ptarmigan that walked about the campsite and clucked a lullaby while we were in our tents. A south wind, which would have been a real boon on the much larger

Henik Lake, helped us the next day as we swung north. A portage of a few hundred yards took us north to an unnamed lake, five miles long and one mile wide, anonymous because nothing distinguishes it from thousands of similar bodies of water in the north country. After crossing an inconspicuous height of land, we came to a bed of boulders and a trickle of water that marked the beginning of the Padlei River, which we would follow for some fifteen miles northward.

Final Days

Paddling Home

CHAPTER 14

Hard Days on the Padlei

Now our way would be steadily downstream, but here the stream was almost nonexistent. We had to manoeuvre the canoe around a continuous jumble of rocks and boulders, often jumping out onto the rocks or into the shallow water to wrestle the craft. Sometimes we walked and guided the canoe with lines. A couple of times we carried half the load across a shallow stretch and then lined the lightened canoe down. Other times we carried everything around a clot of boulders – a mini-portage. "A rock garden," in the lingo of canoeists, is a stretch of rapids filled with rocks, but a distinct flow of water. This stretch of the Padlei, however, did not have that much water – it was just a sinuous track of boulders. The immediate future did not look bright either. The map indicated a couple of hard days ahead, including the unbroken three miles of portaging that George had mentioned in Toronto. The labour of that carry I had tried to put out of my mind, and now it was a looming presence.

We camped in mid-portage on a barren hillside. George had walked ahead to see what the river was like and Gerd had wandered off after they had put up the tents. Dave and I were going about our cooking chores when a dark cloud appeared suddenly from the west. The wind increased drastically and a few peals of thunder crashed – the first of the trip. George and Dave's tent tore loose from most of its pegs. As a brief rain fell, Dave ran over to grab the frame before the tent started to tumble across the tundra. I threw a heavy bag into our tent, which was holding well, and helped Dave. The storm passed as quickly as it had come. Two segments of the aluminum tent frame were so bent as to be unusable, and others needed straightening. We fixed the frame with spares and the tent was soon up again, this time with large rocks weighing down the corners. Only the previous day I had remarked that in Florida there was thunder almost daily in July. George had remarked that we had not yet experienced the ferocious winds of the Northwest Territories. Now we had sampled their sudden fury.

This was our thirty-first camp, and we were about 150 miles from Eskimo Point. My thoughts (and probably the others') were turning towards home. The remaining distance was short compared to the 650 miles so far. I wanted to savour each day, but my return to my family seemed closer and closer, and more in my thoughts.

With the end of the trip approaching, I supposed that I could jettison a piece of equipment that had served me well. The blue sneakers that I wore most of the time had such holes and tears in the canvas that they no longer provided stable footing. Walking in the water and slipping and sliding off rocks had done them in. So I built up the fire and made a funeral pyre for my faithful sneakers, as all four of us took solemn note of their passing. Now I would wear my remaining pair during the day; if I wanted dry footwear for camp it would have to be the much flimsier wetsuit booties.

The footing on this portage is as treacherous as it gets.

The various dishes in our meals generally required no more than a half-hour of cooking, except for beans, which take an hour. Cooking beans is also tedious – they require constant stirring lest they burn, particularly over the uneven heat of an open wood fire. That evening we had beans and I burned them, along with, somehow, a pot of pudding. I felt guilty that Dave had to scrape and scrub those pots when he washed dishes. To crown my triumph, the beans were not uniformly cooked: some portions were burned, while others had the consistency of pebbles.

Another day of following the Padlei turned out to be demanding. We greeted with relief each stretch of water that could be paddled, even 50 yards. Again we walked and hand-guided the canoes; we lined them or portaged them around impassable portions. When walking or even when lining, we were often bent over with both hands on the gunwales to turn the canoe around boulders or to lift it over shallows, using unaccustomed muscles. It was basically stoop labour, with the added feature of feet slipping and sliding over submerged rocks. On this stretch, a portage was a change of pace, but unwelcome, since it was even tougher. An early portage that day was a half-mile of toil over rough rocks and through scrub willow – and in our head nets, owing to the miasma of blackflies.

While working our canoe, I suggested to George that we make a longer day of it than our two previous short and relatively easy days. In contrast to my earlier desire to enjoy the north leisurely, I had now become more eager to return home. George was non-committal, but when we came to a portage a mile long he suggested that I take the canoe across. I could not refuse – he had carried it almost always, and I was grateful. I had rationalized that his 25-pound advantage in weight, and his strength, made this unequal distribution of effort not inappropriate. The canoe's 75 pounds was not much more than the weight of our packs, at least when they were full of food at the beginning of a trip, but carrying the canoe was considerably harder because of the distribution of its weight. The upturned craft sitting on one's shoulders, and extending eight feet forward and eight feet back, called for unusual exertions of upper body, arms and legs. I suspected, and George later agreed, that my "vinegar" in proposing a somewhat longer day had prompted the suggestion.

We prepared for the portage, tucking things away and tying up packs. The day was cloudy and blustery, and the landscape grey and featureless. I tied

126

two paddles between the thwarts, pushed the canoe up over my head with the paddles resting on my shoulders, and set off. But a strong wind was blowing from my left. It caught the craft and exerted a sideways twist. I had to push on the gunwales in the opposite direction and apply torsion in all sorts of directional combinations to maintain my balance. It was a task just to stand upright in the wind, but I also had to walk forward, keeping my footing and balance over the rough ground. I was soon gasping for air and pouring sweat. When George, carrying his pack, took hold of a line from the bow of the canoe to help counteract the twist from the wind, my task eased from intolerable to excruciating. I concentrated on each step – leg, arm, torso muscles in hard use – looking to put each foot down so as to maintain balance as much as possible, finding that footing and then looking to the next one. With my huffing and puffing, existence became that one immediate step. Only in retrospect could I acknowledge that Dave was also carrying a canoe and that the other two men, with their packs, did not have a much easier time of it. To make matters worse, one of my paddles had worked loose during my struggles and was sliding around, destabilizing the load even more until I retied it. The strain must have been evident on my face because George, faithful recorder of events, quickly took a close-up photograph of me when I put the canoe down. Not much else was worth photographing that grey day, when the barren lands deserved their name. I never saw the picture, so I can only imagine how I must have looked after that ordeal.

The portage seemed unending but probably took no more than two hours. When we started paddling for a stretch – what blessed relief! – I was again surprised how rapidly the memory of excruciating labour receded. We discussed how to proceed for the rest of the day. It was 5:00 p.m., and George wanted to stop pretty soon, while the rest of us expressed a mild preference for going for a couple of more hours. George prevailed and we decided to look for a campsite a mile or so downstream. As the other canoe pulled away after our discussion, I said, "George, as a novelty, you should let us have our way some time."

"Yes, but we are not equals on this trip."

"Sure. You're the leader, but we are not just support personnel for your trip either."

"I'm not really doing that, am I?"

I replied with a grin, "Only a little."

We paddled on, but then Dave and Gerd did not pull in to look for a campsite where George had suggested.

"Look at them. Maybe there is a revolt under way," I said.

"Yeah, they are not looking to stop. Maybe you're right."

We landed near the place that George had originally suggested, and Dave and Gerd had to paddle back a quarter-mile to rejoin us. Nothing further was said about where to camp or how far to travel. We had covered eight miles, but with considerable effort. Two rivets had come loose in the hull of our canoe during the hard going of that day, and the cumulative wear and tear of five weeks was taking its toll. George patched the craft in short order, but he had not mentioned the repair as a reason for the early stop. I had known George a long time and was at ease with his leadership, but I suspected that some resentment might be brewing. No overt signs of tension appeared that evening as we went about our camp chores, but in the morning David was curt and sharp, and he complained about my burned pots of two evenings earlier. When George asked him whether he wanted to walk to the top of a small hill under which we were camped to look over our way ahead, David snapped, "Definitely not!" So George went alone, and we broke camp.

A swatch of white on the southern slope of the hill on the opposite bank of the river aroused my curiosity. It was a snowbank and it reminded us, on this twenty-eighth day of July, that we were in the far north. It was protected from the prevailing winds that help melt snow and evidently was deep enough to have lasted this far into the summer. It probably survived until new snow fell.

A five-mile paddle through a broad lake-like segment of the river provided an easy start to the day, but we knew that it would soon end. When the river bowed westward through what the map indicated was a series of rapids, we climbed out and started the single longest portage of the expedition. We cut across a height of land to the east of the river, intending to rejoin it shortly before it emptied into Kinga Lake, after a carry of almost three miles. One blessing was that our packs were relatively light, since we had consumed quite a bit of food. But the canoes were as heavy as always, having deposited only ounces of aluminum on various rocks along the way.

Peter and Gerd part way on the three-mile portage around the "mighty" Padlei River.

We went first across a meadow of grassy hummocks, between which we picked our way, and then, on higher ground, over fairly smooth rock. Portaging was always an ordeal and we knew that this would be a long one. After the first dozen steps, the pack settled into the shoulders, our leg and back muscles strained with each step, and our neck muscles pushed the forehead against the tumpline. Gravity transferred each ounce of the load, painfully, to the body. I slogged on and resented each rise in elevation and cursed each obstacle, whether bush, boulder or mud. We just keep humping our packs. We were tough by then, but the carry was still sweaty labour.

We took the first load of packs close to two miles before stopping on a hill about a mile east of the river. We had left the canoes for the next round, when we would have a better idea of the route. When I released myself from the pack, I felt as if I would float away. In the distance a grey swath of boulders marked the course of the river through the tundra; hardly any water was visible. I pointed to it and exclaimed, "Behold the mighty Padlei!" We propped a paddle upright to mark the first load and returned for the canoes and the other packs. This time we pursued what the view from the hill had indicated was a more direct route, and we headed even further east. About halfway we stopped to rest and to swap loads. The wind again was strong enough to require the person not carrying the canoe to help straighten it from the front. Eventually we neared our destination on the river's bank, and I already felt better. We descended the hill to some willows along the now smoothly flowing river. For a moment we rested and enjoyed the lush grassy riverside in the noonday sun, then we trekked back for the other packs.

Eating lunch and lying about on the grass afterwards – only a few mosquitoes were about – we patted ourselves on the back. I said, "Now that we have worked like mules and done this carry, we can feel like stallions," which drew a few satisfied chuckles. The ordeal had not been as bad as I had feared. As is frequently the case, the prospect was worse than the reality.

After the utter barrenness of the previous three days, the grassy banks and yellowish-green marshes of the final portion of the Padlei River welcomed us to Kinga Lake. At the very entrance to the southeastern end of the lake, the Padlei did remind us of its heritage because we faced some rapids, but we easily walked the canoes through that rock garden. The sun shone on wooded shores and sandy beaches that nestled beneath the bald, rocky hills surrounding the lake. We had descended some 150 feet in three miles, and spruce and tamarack abounded in this sheltered region – lush and pastoral, in contrast to the barren high ground. A weathered cabin in a bay to the west attracted us. Made of sawn lumber, rather than of more readily available logs, it nestled next to a brook that bubbled down from the high ground and then wound its way through a meadow to the lake. The deserted structure overlooked the meadow and sinuous stream in the foreground, and the view stretched across the lake to a prominent hill in the east. An idyllic spot had attracted the builder – probably someone connected to the abandoned Hudson's Bay Company post a few miles across the lake in its northwest corner.

We paddled to that old post, going around a peninsula and then to the west end of the lake, where the Maguse River enters. Five white buildings, with the company's characteristic red roofs, sat on a hillside near the shore. Someone had painted the alternative spelling – Padley Post – on a large rock in front. We clambered out to look around. George, who is particularly interested in historical sites and northern settlements, did a careful canvas. The buildings baked in the sun; all was silent, save for the wind soughing. The open, empty structures spoke of the people and the trading that had gone on there – of traders, usually Scots, leading lonely lives at the post and dealing with the Inuit or occasional Chipewyan up from the interior as they passed through. Some indigenous people settled near the posts for extended periods. I thought also of the starvation among the Inuit when the Canadian government resettled them here in the early 1950s, captured by the pictures in Harrington's *The Face of the Arctic*. Two distinct rubbish heaps, one of rusty tin cans and the other of chalky caribou bones, spoke of the two cultures that met here.

I am not much for musty buildings, so after a look around I withdrew to a sunny spot out of the wind, clutching a paperback that I had found in one of the houses. New reading material was welcome, even something as forgettable as that book. I read and dozed for an hour while the others went about their pursuits. Enough mosquitoes were buzzing about to make me put up the hood of my jacket. I lay in the grass, looking out across Kinga Lake and beyond, to the rolling ground that hid the Padlei River. I thought about our trip, about all we had done; we had come a long, hard way. Behind me stood old outposts of civilization, now unused, and in my hand was a book. I belonged to the life of books and buildings, but the north – serene and abiding, water and tundra stretching seemingly forever – was enchanting. I forgot about what I was reading and looked out on the lake and the barren lands, knowing that we would soon leave. And so we spent a leisurely afternoon. Then we paddled eastward five miles across Kinga Lake and camped where the Maguse River leaves the lake.

Everyone was in a good mood. We had finished the long portage; the rest of the trip seemed straightforward. We wondered a bit about the severity of the rapids that awaited us on the Maguse River, but we did not expect any real difficulty in the approximately 100 miles of downriver paddling to Hudson Bay. At the very end of the expedition we would have to cover twenty miles of open sea along Hudson Bay – a prospect that gave me pause because of tides and possible winds. But I put aside those concerns. They were still a few days away, and we would worry about them when we discovered what the conditions actually were like. Instead we talked about finishing the journey and started to anticipate our return to civilization. Most of us looked forward to ice cream and fresh fruit. George mentioned shaving and bathing to prepare for meeting other people. I was eager to see my family, especially little Kristopher who had almost doubled in age since I left. Still, the north and our life there had taken a hold on me and wisps of melancholy drifted through my mind at the prospect of leaving.

CHAPTER 15

Snow Geese and Goslings:
Downriver to Tidewater

Soon after setting out on the Maguse River we encountered
rapids, but easy ones, making the canoeing interesting and speeding
us along. "A friendly river, the Maguse!" I thought, as it emptied into the
north end of Heninga Lake. After paddling a pleasant three or four miles
across the top of the lake, we re-entered the Maguse – more boisterous
here, as more streams fed it. Downstream we saw sheer rock walls, 20 to
30 feet high, and angular granite blocks beneath them, announcing narrow channels and heavy currents. We stopped to look the situation over.
A small rocky islet, about a city lot in area, divided the river into two furi-
ous channels. So we carried everything around the rapids. The going was
good over expanses of flat rock, almost like a sidewalk. Only occasionally
did we have to step carefully from one plate to another.

The map showed a string of rapids on the Maguse, but we could determine their difficulty only by inspection. Sometimes – too rarely from our
perspective – the rapids could be run easily or were so innocuous that we
wondered why they were marked as "rapids." Some do not even appear
on the map. Others are very real, with heavy water leaping about chaot-
ically. Even with our covered canoes we did not consider running three
of them; we debated about a fourth but, since George, our expert,
demurred, we readily hauled our gear around those too. I had been hoping for some easy downhill canoeing, even for some exhilarating rapids
as on the Kognak, but met with disappointment. Portaging is never easy
and is harder yet after hoping to avoid it. The portages were not terribly
difficult or long (all less than a half-mile), but one crossed a jumble of

A typical stretch along the upper and middle Maguse River.

sharp-edged rocks, with many shards pointing up. I scrambled and tottered across it and muttered to myself, "What the hell am I doing here, wandering around like a mountain goat, with a heavy load on my back?" For the second or third time on the trip I thought, "This is insane drudgery, and George is insane to do it almost every summer."

The land on this section of the Maguse was completely barren – mostly rock, with some sand. The only signs of life were Inukshuks placed every two or three miles and the odd pair of sandhill cranes. We saw the birds always in pairs and only in rocky, desolate areas. Loons had become more and more scarce as we had moved north and then had disappeared as we approached the treeline. It was as though the cranes replaced the loons. The rocky banks were devoid of even the most scrubby willow or moss. The entire aspect appeared a grey-blue monochrome – partly cloudy sky, light grey rocks, and dark grey water occasionally boiling into green haystacks and foam.

At one place the view downstream was suddenly ominous as the water level in front of us seemed to disappear. We were about to put ashore on the right-hand side to reconnoitre when George changed his mind and said to put ashore on the left, so we paddled across the current and landed on the rocks. We had crossed above a full-fledged waterfall – a drop of twelve to fifteen feet between vertical walls of very pale grey rock. We had not heard it, as there was fast water behind us and the wind was blowing towards the falls. The geometrical cut of the falls and the lightness of the rock gave the scene a surreal aspect, almost like a line drawing illustration. George said that if he had known what was coming he would not have suggested we cross the current where we did.

Later we ran one set of rapids part way but then lined its last 30 yards, down a current faster and more powerful than any that we had yet lined. The Maguse had gathered even more water from tributaries and, in this stretch, was narrowly channelled. We edged down the right side of the river, keeping the canoe aligned with the current, not letting it slant across the flow, because the current could easily sweep it downstream or overturn it. George kept a very tight hold on the line from the stern and accommodated it to the tension that I was putting on the bowline. The going was as tense as paddling down rapids. A couple of drops or ledges one or two feet high on this stretch called for even more careful work, but the footing was good, as we could work from flat slabs of rock.

When we entered a calm Torquetil Lake under a warm afternoon sun, my mood did not improve. My right Achilles tendon had been bothering me more than usual. Our feet, and associated tendons, were frequently in cold water and being worked while cold. I thought that I had strained the tendon on one of those times and probably aggravated it on the long Padlei portage and then again today. The sun is usually enough to cheer me up, but not that afternoon. Perhaps I was getting worn out, or burned out, and I questioned the whole venture again.

Why would anyone go through these numbing labours and staggering difficulties? Why forgo, even for a few weeks, the comforts of a life that our ancestors have worked for centuries to develop? An immediate answer is that we do it precisely to escape that daily life, to experience novelty and a change of scene – the usual reason for a vacation. But on most travels people seek out comfort; why seek out work and grime, cold and wet? For one thing, on some vacations activity and exertion are specific objectives. A canoeist or backpacker or mountaineer partakes actively not of busy work, but of exertions that are a challenge and – more to the point – essential to safe return, to survival. Of course, to survive is to escape the wild, to return to the civilization deliberately left behind. The trip is clearly unnecessary; nothing external compels it. A wilderness adventure is literally an excursion – a side trip to another world.

Among the satisfactions and pleasures on a voyage is that life there is full of simple, immediate tasks. You paddle or you carry packs and canoes across a portage to move forward; you prepare food; you put up and take down the tent. There are plenty of things to do related to survival and existence. Even if you take along concerns that hovered over you back home, immediate tasks now so completely engage you that those concerns disappear. You live in the present.

People turn to nature, too, for spiritual sustenance (or, perhaps, to recover something that is missing). As Henry David Thoreau observed, "In wildness is the preservation of the world." An experience of nature can be a resurrection. It can come in small doses – from gazing at a mountain meadow or sauntering in a forest for an afternoon – but an extended journey into the wilderness and living intimately in the land permits not only a more intense experience, but one that differs in quality. By making a more profound commitment to nature's vagaries – by submitting to it, by entering into it – we truly embrace nature and become close to an essential part of ourselves. To speak of a mystical oneness with nature may be a cliché, but I can describe the sense of well-being that I rapidly came to feel in the north (despite the hardships) only as that which comes with feeling profoundly at ease, connected to the matrix in which I found myself.

A wilderness experiences is liberating. It produces the very comforting knowledge that you can survive wild nature, that you can even relish it, that you are not dependent on artifacts or social structures, no matter how wonderful and useful they are. You feel that you can not only survive but also do reasonably well in the wilderness, even when the elements do not align with your plans. You sever dependencies and establish, or re-establish, other connections – to the immediate surroundings which, in their stark and pristine serenity, are as abiding and real as can be. And there also seems to be a more primordial connection – to the earth, to our essential roots. In the wilderness you are not dependent, not hanging passively from some support system, but rather vitally connected to your matrix.

Paddling allows for, even seems to call for, all sorts of ruminations but, no matter what thoughts drifted through our heads, we always pushed on. After paddling seven miles across the width of the lake, we made camp in the bay of a long, narrow peninsula made up of one long esker. The prospect of starting the next morning with a portage, albeit a short one, across the peninsula did not do much to improve my spirits. We were on a gently curving sandy beach that sloped gradually up to the top of the esker. Caribou signs – tracks and trails – abounded; a solitary critter had scuttled off over the hill as we had landed. In contrast to the channel of the Maguse through which we had passed earlier, here not a rock was in sight, and sand stretched forever. The air was still and sultry. The presence of a palm or two would have made the place seem tropical. Instead open, treeless country lay all around us, with ground cover here and there and brown amber sand curving north and south into the distance. Everything glowed in the soft, golden light that came directly from the setting sun and also, by reflection, from the expanse of lake to the west.

Resting in the mellow light beside the glassy smooth lake, I found that my spirits began to lift. I again felt at ease with my surroundings. The mosquitoes, which were enjoying the evening so forcibly that I put on my head net, did not dispel the mood. (This was the first time I had donned the head net in a week.) The drink of rum that David offered also helped. I sat on the beach and wrote in my log. David was also writing and busying himself with his pack and, while George went off to take photographs, Gerd somewhat nervously set about his first stint of cooking – a pot of beef Stroganoff – on our little gas stove. The beach had no wood for a fire except for small bits of driftwood that we could have gathered to make a skimpy fire.

✳   ✳   ✳

The next day continued calm, bright and still surprisingly warm. We were at a latitude of almost 62°N starting to veer slightly southward as we headed east. The thermometer read 86°F in the direct sun, of which there was plenty, and 74°F in the shade, of which there was none. By now we were quite used to having no trees in view – just water and rolling hills clad in green ground cover or dun rocks.

We had romped across the country because of extraordinarily good conditions and our willingness to work hard. In fact, we were a week ahead of schedule, even after the three extra days on our excursion towards Windy Lake.

We had lunch on a hilltop about 150 feet above water level. A few caribou antlers were lying around. I pointed to a caribou skull with antlers attached and said, "Look, guys, this caribou shed its skull along with its antlers." Gerd paused to consider this and noticed three spent .222 Remington shells stuck on the tines of the antlers. Inuit hunters had used the spot as a campsite or, more probably, as a place for lunch and for dressing the caribou that they had bagged. We were definitely in Inuit country, what with frequent sightings of tent rings in the good camping spots and Inukshuks on the banks of the river every three miles or so.

Inukshuks are piles of rocks, with usually a large one on the bottom and two or three smaller ones stacked on top of it. Occasionally we saw a more elaborate construction. In this relatively featureless landscape they are visible from long distances and serve as guideposts or markers. Their purpose might also be to habituate caribou to human-like profiles so that they do not frighten when a hunter appears. I liked to think that an Inukshuk might be just a gesture stating that a human being passed this way through the lonely land.

I had attempted to fish three or four times and had caught only some pike – a poor treat compared to lake trout – and I thought that on a trip such as this I should be able to claim that I caught lake trout. So I trolled while we paddled and caught two small trout and lost a third when I tried to land it. It broke the line and swam off, with the red and white lure hanging from its mouth. Gerd, our most avid fisherman, also caught two. In camp that evening, on another gravelly esker, I set out to make a fish chowder. It turned into a communal effort. Gerd offered to clean the four fish. Dave diced a fresh onion, left over from our social day at the head of Henik Lake, and did the same for one pound of canned bacon – the ingredient that produced our delicious chowders. He also undertook to start the gas stove, saying that he had one like it. But in priming it he sloshed gas over the stove and, when he lit it, the stove was enveloped in flames. I hoped the gas tank would not explode. In the previous few days, because the expedition was winding down and he still had most of a quart of rum left, Dave had started a cocktail hour. I was glad to participate and George did too, but Gerd remained faithful to beer, even if none was available. This time it looked as though Dave might have overdone things. He did acknowledge that he felt clumsy from his generous libation.

While I cooked the chowder and dessert, the other three bathed. I was not moved to join them. The chowder was, as always, a delicious change of pace. Everyone devoured copious amounts and exclaimed at the treat. George's compliment took the form of, "Peter, remember who taught you how to make chowder."

Afterwards, replete, we lolled about like elephant seals and digested. David fell asleep, with his head up on a mossy rise, looking very comfortable in the evening sun. Even better, a breeze sprang up and chased the mosquitoes away. To make a more cheery campsite as dusk settled in, I prepared a small fire with driftwood gathered from the beach.

I had collected the wood on the way back from carrying out, as P.G. Downes says, "one of the humbler functions." This activity is easier with the proper technique – facing one's backside into a stiff breeze, which we now had. If a breeze is not available, then one has to choose between a backside bitten by mosquitoes and blackflies or a function hurried and even more graceless than usual.

The wind gained strength during the night, buffeting the tent and making sleep difficult.

The south wind continued in the morning. We paddled two miles with it at our side before we gave up and went to ground at a low point on the southwest side of Maguse Lake. During our paddle of the previous day, the river had widened into a lake – long, irregular, from two to five miles wide and stretching for more than forty miles from northwest to southeast, with plenty of bays and islands. We lay about behind scrub willows, trying to stay out of the wind; people dozed, read or wrote in their diaries. A lone caribou, shaggy and gaunt, trotted unconcerned between our canoes and us, no more than ten yards away.

After four hours the wind diminished and we resumed paddling. David, evidently restless and eager to finish, suggested that we push on that day and get off Maguse Lake – an unrealistic proposal, since some thirty miles still faced us. George said that he was not in that much of a rush, which set him and David off into a bit of an argument about priorities. Gerd and I stayed out of it. I surmised that George wanted to savour more of the north, particularly since we were well ahead of schedule. I certainly felt that way too – who knew when I would again be paddling a wild northern river?

Nearing tidewater on the Maguse.

But the landscape was changing. It became ever more featureless as we approached the coastal plain. The river had become wider; its formerly steep banks now merged imperceptibly with a background as flat as if it had been levelled by a giant bulldozer. But the glacier had not swept away everything; it had left behind rocks and boulders, scattered randomly. In the monotonous landscape the Inukshuks were a particularly welcome sight. The map said that we still had to descend 158 feet to sea level – a surprisingly large drop over the 35 or so miles to Hudson Bay. But the low, flat aspect announced a coastal plain and the final segment of our journey. After the wind died, the afternoon and evening were again sunny and warm, almost balmy, but now I did not feel at ease in the low, featureless barrens. The land seemed to belong to the sea, as if it could be reclaimed with a healthy tide and as if we were allowed on it at sufferance. Perhaps the wasteland of scattered rocks, perhaps the imminence of the open sea and the end of the trip, put me off. At 7:00 p.m. we made camp on a small, low island.

*   *   *

We fought a stiff wind again the next morning. At noon we reached the end of the lake and found the shelter of the river channel. While eating lunch we saw Inuit in a large motorized canoe in mid-river. Then another canoe came by, and I knew that our trip was nearing its end. Cranes and snow geese were about in numbers. The fluffy goslings again tempted us and we caught a couple and no doubt terrified them before we let them go. The Maguse does make a swift run to the sea here, down a trough-like channel between gravelly, rocky banks. Every now and then a small patch of grass appeared on the beige banks, frequently decorated with small purple flowers that stuck an inch up above the grass. The rapids, for the most part, were inconsequential; they just moved us along at a great pace. We did come to some abrupt shelves that marked the beginning of more serious rapids. George and I landed on the left and made a short carry, while the other canoe managed to make it down the right side with some lining.

We made an early camp at 5:30 p.m., having covered some 32 miles despite the morning wind on the lake, but with the great help of the swift current. Since this was our last night of camping, I insisted on a wood fire, so David went to some trouble and gathered a large bunch of willows. They burn even while green. I also gave George the four bars of chocolate-covered marzipan that I had been saving for his birthday, and we had that as an extra treat for dessert. His birthday was still a few days away, but I thought that we would appreciate the marzipan more in the wild than back in civilization – and we did. It was hard to believe that we would be in a town the next evening – a notion that competed for my attention with the prospect of canoeing on the open waters of Hudson Bay.

CHAPTER 16

White Canvas Tents on Hudson Bay

THE LAST DAY ARRIVED – AT least, it would be the last one if everything went well – and I felt that the others shared my excitement.
Perhaps they also shared my wistfulness at journey's end. We would no
longer be as independent of anyone or anything outside our little party.
In the city we would have comforts that approach the voluptuous, and
they might become routine, but I would not feel the vital connection to
my surroundings that I do in the wild.

On the trip there was always another bend in the river, a new vista, a
new task that demanded attention, or at least effort. This time, we saw
two white canvas tents as we approached the tidal flats. We felt no exul-
tation about having reached the sea. Hudson Bay was just grey, rolling
waves in the distance under a similarly hued sky. We stopped and were
surrounded by four or five children. Soon two people – a couple in the
late twenties – came out from their tent and invited us in for coffee, if we
brought our own cups. They had a year-old baby and five-year-old daugh-
ter, who held back a bit and stared but soon asked questions of the strangers
from upriver. The parents were teachers who had spent the previous year
on Baffin Island and had committed themselves to jobs at Eskimo Point
(now called Arviat) for at least a year. Greg was Caucasian and Nancy was
Inuit. Nancy said that it was quite rare, at that time, for a native Inuit
speaker to be a teacher in an Inuit community. Most of the teachers were
white, came for a year, then left. Greg sported a couple of Nikon cameras
and all sorts of lenses. He also wore a heavy parka, insulated coverall pants
and an assortment of rain gear. The Inuit, in contrast, had on light parkas
or windbreakers. We chatted and drank coffee around their Coleman stove,

which seemed to me to keep their tent oppressively warm.

We questioned them at some length about their lives, but I neglected to find out how they, two teachers with two young children, handle child care. Probably the community provides it in some informal way, as a matter of course, as I had read. I saw Pampers in the tent, and there had been used ones outside. We learned that their baby was allergic to milk and had to drink a special preparation.

They had attended Lakehead University in Thunder Bay, Ontario. In their married life, they had travelled extensively – to Europe, California, Florida and other places in the United States. Greg's mother lived near Fort Lauderdale, Florida, and I wondered whether there was anyone who did not have a parent or grandparent living in Florida. Nancy, charming and lively, articulated the problems of indigenous peoples in North American culture. She was determined to maintain Inuit culture for her children but realized how difficult it would be in the face of TV and consumerism. She wanted, at least, to raise their children in the north until they were of school age.

They and another family were camped at the mouth of the Maguse for a weekend outing. After talking with us for an hour, the two families got into their motor-driven freighter canoes and headed upriver to hunt caribou. We remained on shore and waited for the east wind to die down so that we could venture out onto Hudson Bay for the final stretch to Eskimo Point. George spent some of the time building a very elaborate Inukshuk, about four feet high and constructed with at least twenty stones, almost a memorial to our trip. Eventually two canoes filled with successful hunters came downriver and landed near us to see what was happening. We talked; they enjoyed our candy and left as we resumed our wait. About 6:30 p.m. another pair of freighter canoes, with two hunters in each, stopped. We gave up on the idea of finishing under our own power and accepted a ride from them.

Each of our seventeen-foot canoes went up on top of the thwarts in one of their large craft. Their canoes are about twenty feet long and four feet deep and wide – much larger than ours, but crowded once loaded. I sat on one of our packs with my legs over a caribou carcass. One of the Inuit loaned me a pair of rubberized overalls to keep off the caribou blood and ocean spray. The canoe also held a couple of wooden boxes of camping gear, two rusty rifles lying on a wet tarpaulin and the remnants of a meal – caribou venison, noodles, a hunk of bacon and a hunting and a butchering knife, all in a large aluminum pot. The best English speaker, Luke, was in the other boat and, since the two Inuit in our boat spoke hardly any English, we did not try to talk over the motor's racket.

We rode a mile out from shore and thundered down the bay. Motoring through the waves, without regard for the wind, felt strange and deflating, even humiliating. The grand finish of our canoe trip was being hauled by motorboat, like some flabby tourists. But I was ready to embrace the comforts of civilization and did not worry too much about it. It turned out that Luke's brother owned a truck, which we engaged to move our gear from the dock to the Eskimo Point airfield. No more portaging for us. We asked what we owed for the motorboat trip and were told, "Whatever you think." When we inquired about the truck, they again replied, "Whatever you think." Was this a clever bargaining technique? Or was I perhaps returning to the cynicism of the city, almost before I was ashore?

During the canoe ride, David had engineered with Luke a trade of his own Grumman paddle for an untanned caribou skin. The rest of us were immediately interested in such a souvenir and had three other skins brought to the airport, to exchange for our plastic and aluminum Mohawk paddles. Then David asked about other items. As a result, he, George and I travelled in the truck back to town so that Dave could try on some caribou-skin robes at Luke's house. He bought a caribou parka by offering "whatever you think." When we eventually took our skins to a tannery in Toronto, we found that they were so eaten by weevils that they were not worth tanning. Maybe David's robe turned out better.

Luke's family did give us a five-gallon container of river water for our camp at the airport. The town does have a reservoir, but this family of hunters preferred river water. The community has just over 1,000 people, many of them children. People lived in closely spaced frame and plywood houses. The streets were dirt and gravel, and almost no grass or anything green was visible. The women wore summer parkas, which had a hood and the standard narrow flap down the front and a broader one over the seat. They used the hoods for carrying children papoose-style. Most residents rode three-wheeled all-terrain vehicles everywhere – from home to store, to visit neighbours, and out into the tundra.

We slept in our tents at the airport – a couple of buildings and a long gravel strip. It was windy and quite a lot colder than inland. After breakfast, we went to arrange for the flight south to Churchill and to see more of the town. The two main stores – Hudson's Bay and the Co-op – sell groceries and general merchandise. A smaller competitor sells hardware items such as boat motors, fishing equipment and snacks. Nurses and teachers, such as Nancy and Greg, are sent by the government of Canada to serve the community and frequently stay only one year. Everyone – civil servants and local Inuit – live in government housing, prefabricated homes shipped in by freighter.

The airplane was full, with all twenty seats taken, and the cargo hold was loaded with our two canoes and other packs. I started to resume my life by chatting with the person in the seat next to me. Mrs. Wright, in her forties, was returning to Winnipeg after two days in Eskimo Point. She had dropped off her foster son, 15-year-old Simeon, to spend a couple of weeks with his sister and her family. Wright had looked after the boy since he was two, when he had gone to Winnipeg to be treated for intestinal problems. When he had returned to Eskimo Point two years earlier for a visit, his family had not allowed him back to Winnipeg; but when he later travelled through Winnipeg with another family, he had run away and rejoined Mrs. Wright. Now she had brought him to visit his sister and her family. His mother was in the hospital in Churchill, and his father was not mentioned. According to Mrs. Wright, the family had treated her very well. Her only complaint was that they bought only junk food.

In Churchill we made good connections for the long train ride to The Pas, where our van awaited. The train again crawled over the muskeg. The two Finns we had met on the Thlewiaza River were also on board. They had gone more directly to Churchill and had taken their time. This reunion and the exchanging of accounts of our journeys made the long ride less tedious. Later I tried to sleep in my seat, with little success.

I thought of where I had been and of how I had travelled during the six weeks. The train now did all the work of hauling me southward, at a brisk pace compared to the canoe. I was now out of the wind and cold, but I languished in the stuffy, smelly car. Out on the water, the breezes could play on me and I would be invigorated by the northern air. On the water, I might strain against the current or the wind and curse the rain, but I would not be inert baggage. On the water, I would be propelling myself forward, and I would see what was in the next bay solely by the dint of my own efforts.

Epilogue

ALTHOUGH I LEFT THE NORTH with a wistful sense of loss, at the same time I was ready to embrace my family – to see Alexandra, Julia, Emily, Karl and the not-so-newborn Kristopher, who had tripled in age to three months since I had left. He was a thriving, wiggling tyke. Being reunited with my family was great beyond expression. I also welcomed the luxuries of life in twentieth-century America. To reacquaint myself with plumbing and running warm water, with restaurants serving fine meals and with clean sheets was easy. But amid family and the comforts of city life, I now had something new and dear, something that I did not have before going north. I knew wild nature as never before, and I think that I knew myself better. I felt comfortable about my connection to the north, to my earth.

When I returned to Florida I was startled to see in the mirror an upper body with surprising breadth and definition – a pleasant development certainly, but not the most lasting result of the trip, for the bulk in my shoulders soon enough descended to my waist. What endured longest were memories – of hurtling rapids, serene landscapes and a simple life directly connected to existence. These are memories that can nourish one for a long time, and they also call one back to the north.

I did go back for another similar voyage eight years later with George. That time it was just the two of us. Gerd never returned to the tundra. Dave did return, at least one time, on a solo trip a couple of years after the expedition described in this book. David Berthelet died in January 1998, a victim of cancer in his 57th year. This last journey of his, occurring much too early, is yet another reminder of our fragility. Since our expedition, except for the year he celebrated his twenty-fifth wedding anniversary and one other summer, George has gone on a similar canoe trip every summer, at least four times carrying out long solo voyages.

For some the pull and tug of the north is irresistible. George is certainly a prime example, as was P.G. Downes, the author of *Sleeping Island* – the book which was the inspiration for our trip. The northern travellers might be few but they are ardent, and I now count myself among them. Although it has been fourteen years since I was last in the far north, I still feel the pull to return, to bask in its long golden evenings, and to canoe where there was a big sky on the water and I could see far.

Further Reading

Downes, P.G. *Sleeping Island: The Story of One Man's Travels in the Great Barren Lands of the Canadian North*. 1943. Saskatoon: Prairie Books, 1988.

Harrington, Richard. *The Face of the Arctic: A Cameraman's Story in Words and Pictures of Five Journeys Into the Far North*. New York: J. Schuman, 1952.

Hearne, Samuel. *A Journey from Prince of Wales Fort in Hudson's Bay to the Northern Ocean, 1769, 1770, 1771, 1772*. Look for reprint editions such as Edmonton: Hurtig, 1971.

Mallet, Thierry. *Plain Tales of the North*. New York: privately printed by Revillon Frères, 1925.

Mallet, Thierry. *Glimpses of the Barren Lands*. New York: privately printed by Revillon Frères, 1930.

Marsh, Winifred Petchey. *People of the Willow: The Padlimuit Tribe of the Caribou Eskimo*. Toronto: Oxford University Press, 1976.

McPhee, John. *Coming into the Country*. New York: Farrar, Straus and Giroux, 1977.

Mowat, Farley. *The Desperate People*. Boston: Little, Brown, 1959.

Mowat, Farley. *People of the Deer*. Boston: Little, Brown, 1952.

Slovic, Scott and Terrel Dixon, eds. *Being in the World: An Environmental Reader for Writers*. New York: Macmillan, 1993.

Tyrrell, J.B., ed. *David Thompson's Narrative of His Exploration in Western America, 1784–1812*. Toronto: The Champlain Society, 1916.

Index

About the Author

PETER KAZAKS STUDIED AT McGILL University, Yale University and the University of California, Davis. He was a physics professor and an administrator at New College in Sarasota, Florida, from which he took early retirement. He now lives in Davis, California, and does some teaching and some soccer refereeing. In recent years he has travelled with one or more of his children in the Pacific northwest, Nevada and Utah, but future trips will probably take him to visit his children and grandchildren who are dispersed along the east and west coasts of North America.